THE
SINISTER BEAUTY
OF
Carnivorous Plants

Matthew M. Kaelin

Schiffer Publishing Ltd

4880 Lower Valley Road · Atglen, PA 19310

Designed by Brenda McCallum
Type set in Aphrodite Slim/Abalone

ISBN: 978-0-7643-5098-6
Printed in China

Published by Schiffer Publishing, Ltd.
4880 Lower Valley Road
Atglen, PA 19310
Phone: (610) 593-1777; Fax: (610) 593-2002
E-mail: Info@schifferbooks.com
Web: www.schifferbooks.com

For our complete selection of fine books on this and related subjects, please visit our website at www.schifferbooks.com. You may also write for a free catalog.

Schiffer Publishing's titles are available at special discounts for bulk purchases for sales promotions or premiums. Special editions, including personalized covers, corporate imprints, and excerpts, can be created in large quantities for special needs. For more information, contact the publisher.

We are always looking for people to write books on new and related subjects. If you have an idea for a book, please contact us at proposals@schifferbooks.com.

Other Schiffer books on horticulture:

Anyone for Orchids?, Georgiana Webber, 978-0-916838-12-6

Basic Topiary: A Living Approach, Dean Myers, 978-0-7643-3634-8

Espalier Fruit Trees For Wall, Hedge, and Pergola: Installation, Shaping, Care, Karl Pieber & Peter Modl, 978-0-7643-4488-6

Dedication

Dedicated to my parents, Joan Kaelin and Michael Kaelin,
my aunt and uncle, Barbara and Bob Gormley,
And my dear grandmother, Lillian Leonard, for all the laughter
we have shared over the years.

.

Nepenthes 'H. R. Giger' cultivar.
November 9, 2013

Nepenthes × *dyeriana*
September 9, 2010

Contents

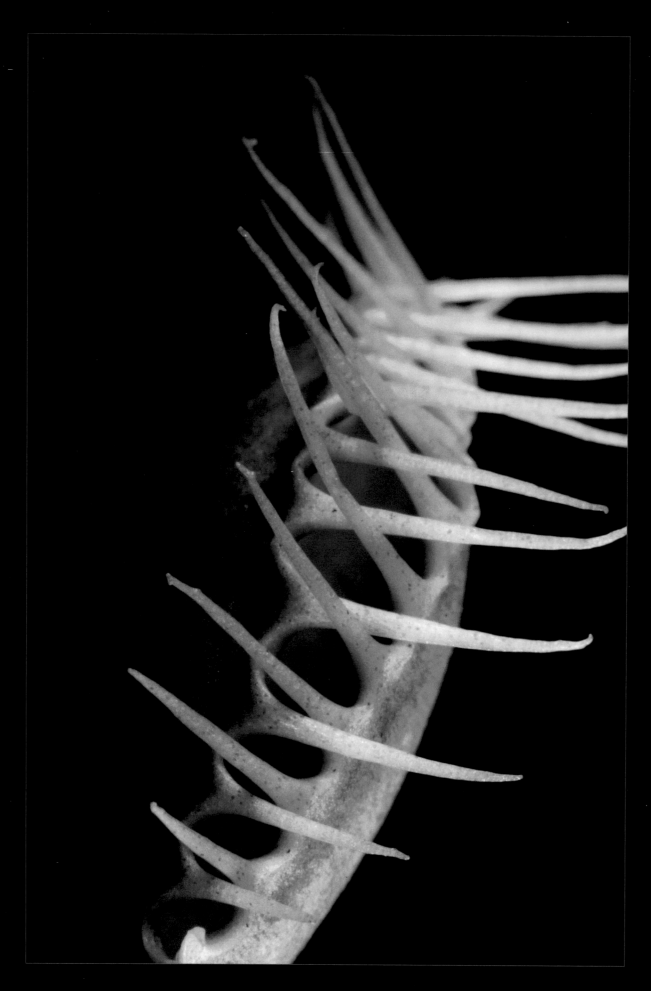

Dionaea muscipula, 'B52' cultivar.
September 5, 2013

Foreword

At the plant nursery I co-own and started in 1989, where we have probably the largest collection of insect- and animal-eating flora on public display in the world, I am frequently asked, "What's your favorite carnivorous plant?" My droll response? "Whichever one I'm looking at!"

This is not far from the truth. Another question I'm often asked is: "Where's Audrey?"

Both of these questions bring me back to my childhood, growing up in the exotic state of New Jersey, living on "the shore" at the edge of the Pine Barrens. A few events happened in rather quick order that changed my life. The first was seeing Roger Corman's 1960 black comedy *The Little Shop of Horrors*, a very funny movie that left such an impression on me I even recall what I was having for dinner at the time: a chicken pot pie. The second event was ordering Venus flytraps advertised in *Famous Monsters* magazine —I was a science-fiction and horror movie fanatic and wanted my own "Audrey Junior," the monster plant who swallowed people whole in Corman's shot-in-two-days film. Those flytraps promptly died.

The third event came that spring, when I volunteered in science class to do a report on the Venus flytrap. A classmate tapped me on the shoulder and told me he knew where Venus "flycatchers" grew. I thought he was crazy—we lived in New "Joisey"!

He took me to the boggy edge of a lake right in the middle of town. He showed me the strangest plants I had ever seen. They weren't Venus flytraps but I was hardly disappointed— they looked like they came from outer space!

I did research in my school's library. I read the fascinating scientific books on carnivorous plants by Charles Darwin (1875) and F. E. Lloyd (1942), but both of these books had primarily line drawings and Lloyd's some crude black and white photos of microscopic details with few of the plants themselves. But what really stunned me was a 1961 article "Plants That Eat Insects" by Dr. Paul Zahl, the most prolific writer and photographer for *National Geographic* magazine. It was the first time beautiful color photographs of carnivorous plants had ever appeared in print. I found out the plants my friend showed me at the lake were purple pitcher plants and sundews. I must have borrowed that magazine dozens of times from the library; I had become obsessed.

Had someone told me half a century ago that a Broadway musical version of *Little Shop of Horrors* would one day be the most frequently produced stage show in America (overtaking the old chestnut *Our Town* in the 1990s, a play I performed in during high school), or that I would one day be friends with Paul Zahl's daughter Eda, featured prominently in his article hand-feeding a doomed insect to a Venus flytrap . . . or that I would become intimate with F. E. Lloyd's grandchildren . . . I would have thought them to be as crazy as the classmate who told me carnivorous plants grew in our Garden State.

Author and photographer Matt Kaelin has also fallen prey to the seductiveness of carnivorous plants, living near the bogs of Long Island, New York, not far from my childhood home. He realizes they are a deadly beauty. The fact that these plants have evolved to lure, catch, kill, and eat insects and small animals is what has made them appear so alien, so strange, and so mesmerizingly beautiful. Matt's photography and public displays of his work have hypnotized many. His work reminds me of a quote about carnivorous plants in an 1849 issue of *Gardeners' Chronicle*: "Can anyone see such marvelous things, knowing them to be only plants, and feel no wonder?"

I hope you enjoy Matt's book as much as I have. Feel the wonder.

Peter D'Amato
The Savage Garden: Cultivating Carnivorous Plants
californiacarnivores.com

Nepenthes lowii × *veitchii.*
June 3, 2015

Prologue

Sex and Death, so intertwined with one another and yet so contradictory, will remain forever imprinted onto the deepest recesses of our human subconsciousness for us to obsess over all eternity. It is this dynamic, the sensual attraction and the sinister nature, that carnivorous plants possess, that is perhaps the reason we find such fascination in them. Their deviant habits utterly foreign to our concept of the natural order of the world, they have been thought throughout history to exist only in myths and in legends—attracting, catching, and consuming everything from microscopic organisms to insects, amphibians, reptiles, and sometimes even rodents, and devouring their prey using various diabolical methods, while exhibiting the most exquisite and macabre beauty.

Many are familiar with the famous Venus flytrap, yet few know that there are more than 730 species in about sixteen genera contained in five orders for carnivorous plants throughout the world, although these numbers can vary as there is some controversy about how one defines the plants that are considered carnivorous. For instance, most of these plants produce their own digestive enzymes to break down their prey, but some depend upon mutualistic symbiotic relationships with predatory insects, protozoa, or bacteria to dissolve and process the victims that they capture. The generally accepted definition of carnivorous plants describes those that have evolved trapping mechanisms to capture and kill prey for the intention of deriving nutrients from them. They have turned to these wicked ways in order to obtain elements like nitrogen, calcium, and phosphorus, which are unavailable in the habitats where they grow, such as in *Sphagnum* bogs, rainforest treetops, and tropical rock-face cliffs.

There is also a common misconception that all carnivorous plants are closely related to one another. In fact, for these plants, the strategy of carnivory has developed independently at least five different times throughout history by way of convergent evolution. Some carnivorous plants are more closely related to what we would call normal, more mundane plants than to the other carnivores.

Wide ranges of diversity can be seen in the carnivorous plants found all across the world, from the jungles of Borneo to the suburbs of North Carolina. Sometimes they are found deep in the wilderness, other times along the sides of roads. They can be seen high in the mountains or near the sea in freshwater seeps of sandy soil. The climates can be hot and wet, cool and humid, completely underwater, or sometimes even dry and alkaline. Indeed, these plants are found on every continent except for Antarctica and can be seen on many of the islands scattered across the globe.

This collection of photographs exhibits the exotic hybrids and rare species of carnivorous plants that I have been personally cultivating for over the last thirteen years. Not all of the various genera of carnivorous plants are represented here, only those I have grown and photographed. Successful cultivation of these plants has given me the ability to determine through experienced observation the best time of the year and the optimum moment of growth for capturing the best possible specimen in a photograph. Only the purest and most flawless subjects are selected. They are chosen when their development is at the height of perfection, when their colors and forms are fully developed but before the traps begin to decline and wither as new ones grow to replace them. The photography is designed so that the observer's eye falls directly on the point of the subject where the viewing is meant to begin. The focal length is deep, so the rest of the image falls into place from the original point of focus, and the eye is to follow this course. This creates depth and dimensionality to make the subject appear robust and alive. The lighting is carefully controlled to prevent reflections or glares on the plant surfaces. Too much light will wash out the vivid colors of these plants and create hot spots that appear as white voids. Too little light will make the photographs appear dull, cold and lifeless. It is important to have the perfect amount, and to consider the

best direction and angles when it comes to the lighting. This brings a sense of atmosphere and creates the effect of chiaroscuro, the contrast between illumination and shadow that accentuates the volume of the form. Clearly defined visions are created by setting the plants against empty backgrounds, which produces a visual weight for each subject and results in negative spaces forming around them. Positive and negative space are balanced with one another for harmony while the subjects themselves encroach upon the edges of the frame to build a subtle tension, creating an impression that is both sensible and unsettling.

Tightly constraining the subjects in their space brings the observer into the world of the plants from the viewpoint of their prey. The prey are consciously absent, accentuating the purity and the perfection of the form, while at the same time depicting their hunger, making them appear as if they are ready to lunge out and attack the viewer.

These lavish images represent the characteristics of the specimens, providing detailed examples for the identification of many carnivorous plants from around the world, yet are much more than a series of static botanical profiles. The compositions are arranged to simulate a sense of movement and life, and so this is a series of living creatures that exist not in some other dimension, but right here in our own. The portrait photography captures the respective traits and personalities of each subject's unique carnivorous adaptations. The macro photography creates alien landscapes that appear exotic and hostile, and yet are strangely alluring. All of these elements fuse together to create an intensity that is most unconventional for the botanical imagery seen in the world today.

The studio photography is done well after sunset to ensure complete darkness, which is necessary for the complete control of the lighting. Simple clamp light fixtures with full-spectrum 60 watt incandescent bulbs are used for the studio lighting and are carefully positioned to shine into a light tent. The light tent does an excellent job of diffusing glare and reflected light, which the surfaces of plants are prone to producing. A Canon EOS50D DSLR camera is used on a tripod with most often an F22 aperture set with a slow shutter speed to compensate so that a great depth of field can be attained. The smallest of the macro photographs sometimes have shutter speeds that approach thirty seconds. The lens normally used for the photography is a Canon 50mm F/1.4 lens. For most of the macro photography, the 50mm lens is combined with a set of macro tubes made by Kenko. When taking the macro photographs, the focus will often be set to the maximum and the camera tripod will be moved slightly forward or backward to achieve the proper focus. Photographs before 2010 were taken using a Canon PowerShot SD 750 and photographs before 2009 were done without the benefit of the light tent. Capturing these unique images did not require high-end equipment, but rather patience and the proficient application of sound photography techniques.

This project also involves local nature conservation and field botany as well. There are sixteen species of carnivorous plants that are native to Long Island, New York, where I live. The historical botanical records of New York have been referenced and selected populations and habitats have been surveyed, in many cases for the first time since the early 1980s. Comparisons have been made between the observed present-day conditions and the historical records for an understanding of the current status and the past health of Long Island's carnivorous plants and their ecosystems. Notably, Long Island contains the only populations of *Drosera filiformis* in New York, mostly on protected lands. Their current status in New York appears to be stable, but the records show that they have been much reduced in the past 100 years. This survey has helped ascertain the vitality of these populations and those of other local carnivorous plants, making it possible to determine the projected requirements for their long-term survival. During this survey, I also discovered three populations of the hybrid sundew, *Drosera × belezeana* (*Drosera rotundifolia × Drosera intermedia*), found for the first time in the State of New York.

All of these findings have been passed on and added to the records of the New York Natural Heritage Program, a partnership between the New York State Department of Environmental Conservation and the State University of New York College of Environmental Science and Forestry. While observing these specimens in the wild, the plants have been photographed to record and characterize them within their natural habitats. They are brought to life by using the available natural lighting to add elements of chiaroscuro, and by visually isolating the subjects from their surrounding environments for the creation of bold compositions. Doing so also clearly identifies the plant's morphological characteristics for the interest of botanical purposes. The outdoor nature photography is opposite in many ways to the indoor studio photography, while they both retain a similar visual aesthetic. The determining factor for the greatest photographs in both the studio and the outdoors is the lighting. In the studio all of the elements are under complete control; the lighting can be adjusted and the subject can be moved to create the desired illumination and composition. On the other hand, in the outdoors all control is lost, and I must adapt to the environmental conditions present. Here it is the time of year and the position of the sun that determines the lighting on the subject. These factors also decide the angle to shoot from and, in turn, roughly govern the composition of the subject. If the angle proves too undesirable, my choice is to wait until the sun has moved to a different position, or return another day at an earlier hour for another, different angle of lighting. My personal preference is warm afternoon light in the early summer, with clear blue skies and intermittent white clouds. As the clouds pass over the sun, great lighting is achieved by waiting until just the right moment to shoot the photograph and also by creatively using the shade of nearby objects to offset the late-day sun.

My natural-habitat studies of carnivorous plants are an ongoing adventure; there are still many more locations to be explored, with many more discoveries to be made. Overall this endeavor has been for the great love of carnivorous plants and is as much about growing these bizarre creatures through careful cultivation as it is about photographing them with creative techniques. Involved are the elements of fine art, horticulture, science, and conservation, merging these various disciplines together into one natural history collection. Carnivorous plants are still little understood or explored, and so this work provides a perspective into this extraordinary world that is aesthetic, informative, and enlightening for all to enjoy.

Drosera filiformis in coastal plains pond shore habitat.
June 14, 2015.

The Carnivorous Plants

The plate index for the images in this chapter
is found starting on page 137.

PLATE 01

RAVENOUS PATIENCE

September 30, 2012

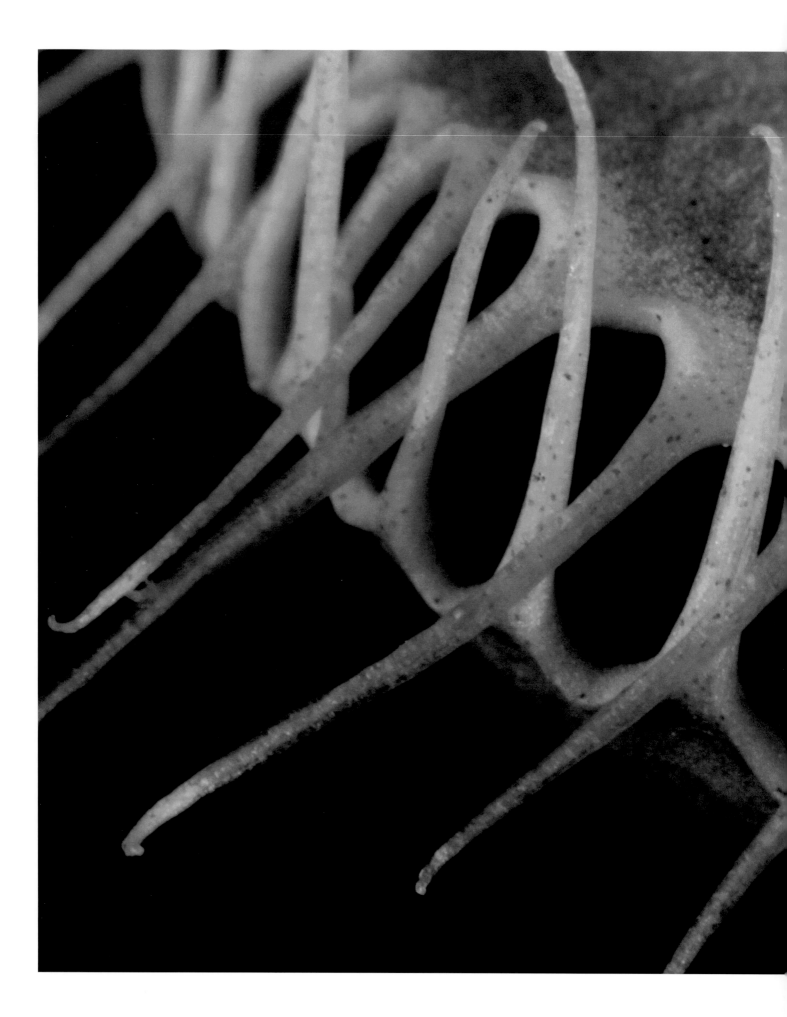

PLATE 02
GNASH
September 5, 2013

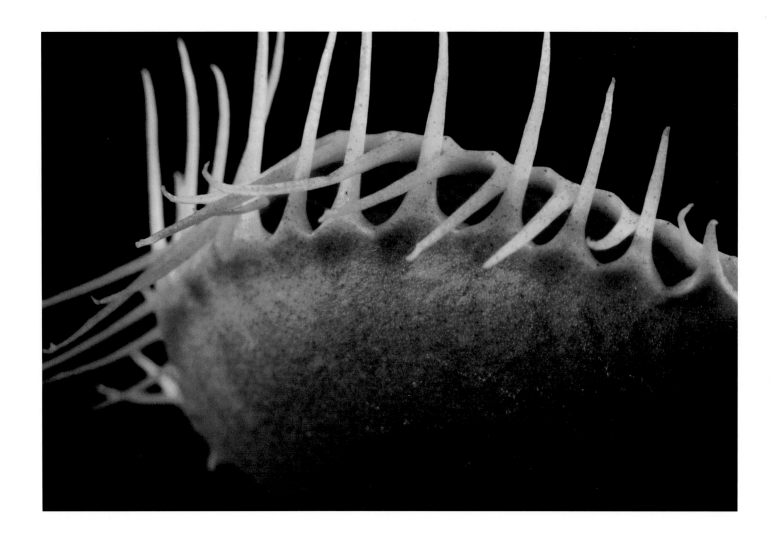

PLATE 03
GLUTTON SWALLOW

September 5, 2013

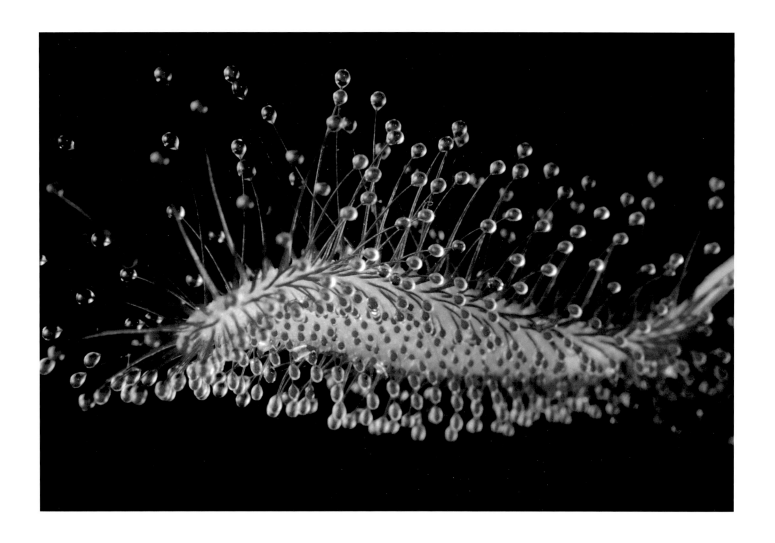

PLATE 04

ONE THOUSAND EYES WATCHING

October 26, 2010

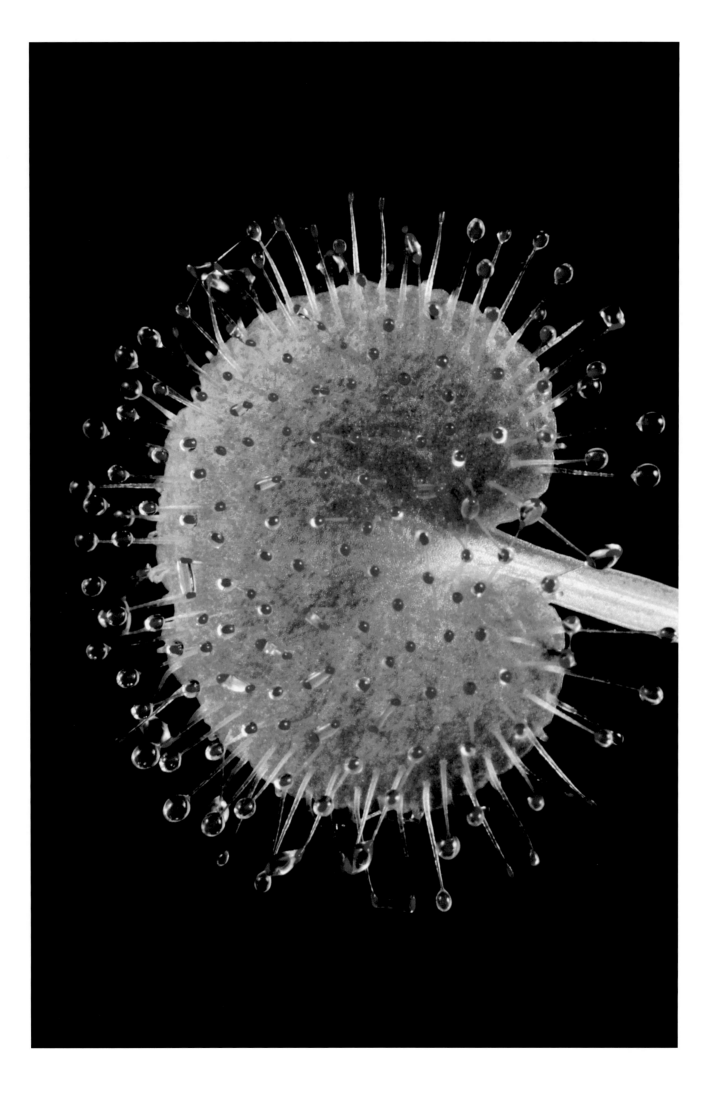

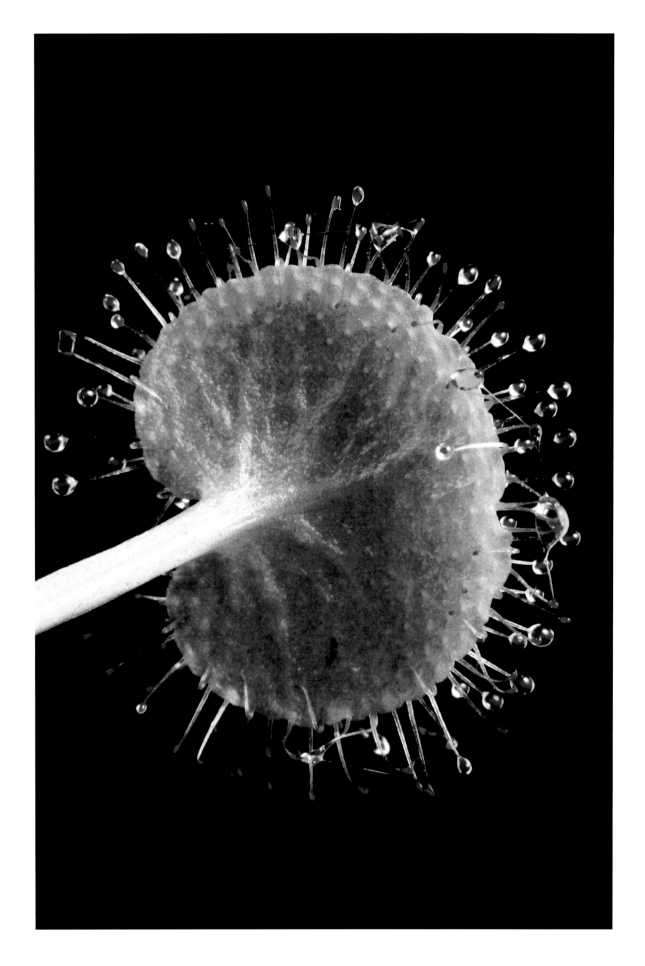

NIGHTMARES FLOAT IN THE SUBCONSCIOUS MIND

October 26, 2013

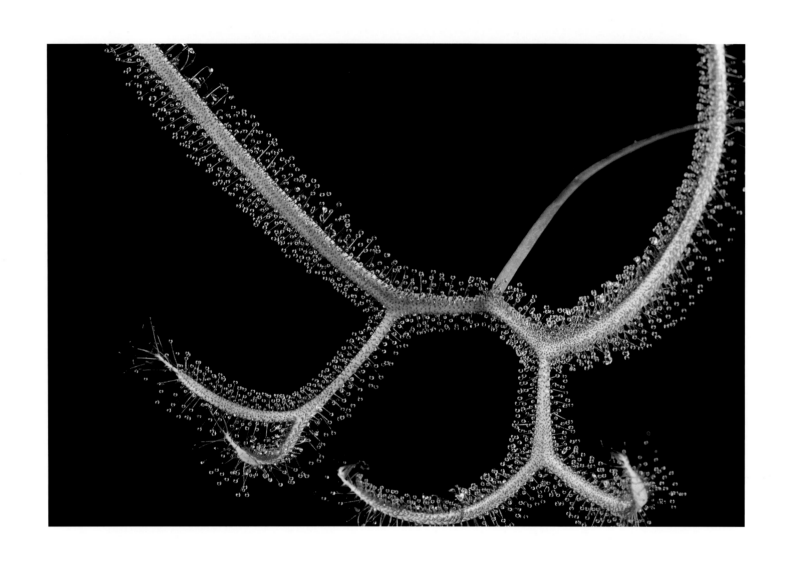

PLATE 07

IN THE GRASP OF THAT OF WHICH IS WICKED

April 15, 2012

PLATE 08
MANIFESTATION OF THE HORRORS BEYOND OUR UNDERSTANDING
September 4, 2010

PLATE 09
HYPNOTIC MASSIVE OPPRESSION
June 9, 2013

PLATE 10

TEMPEST

October 18, 2014

PLATE 11
THRASHING WRITHE IN BLISSFUL TORMENT

September 6, 2013

PLATE 12
TRUTH WITHIN BRILLIANT HALLUCINATIONS

October 21, 2012

PLATE 13

SUPPLE FLESH TO RIPPLE WET

October 21, 2012

PLATE 14
SPITE'S SINGULAR PURPOSE IS REVENGE

October 21, 2012

PLATE 15
WHAT BRINGS THE VISCOUS OOZE

October 21, 2012

PLATE 16
SEETHING EDGE
OF CHAOS
February 15, 2014

PLATE 17
DESCENT INTO THE ABYSS
October 28, 2012

PLATE 18
THE MOLOCH MUST BE OBEYED
February 15, 2014

PLATE 19
UNSEEN GRIMACE BEHIND A FACELESS VISAGE

October 28, 2012

PLATE 20
SKULKING INTENTIONS EMBODIED IN FORM

June 13, 2011

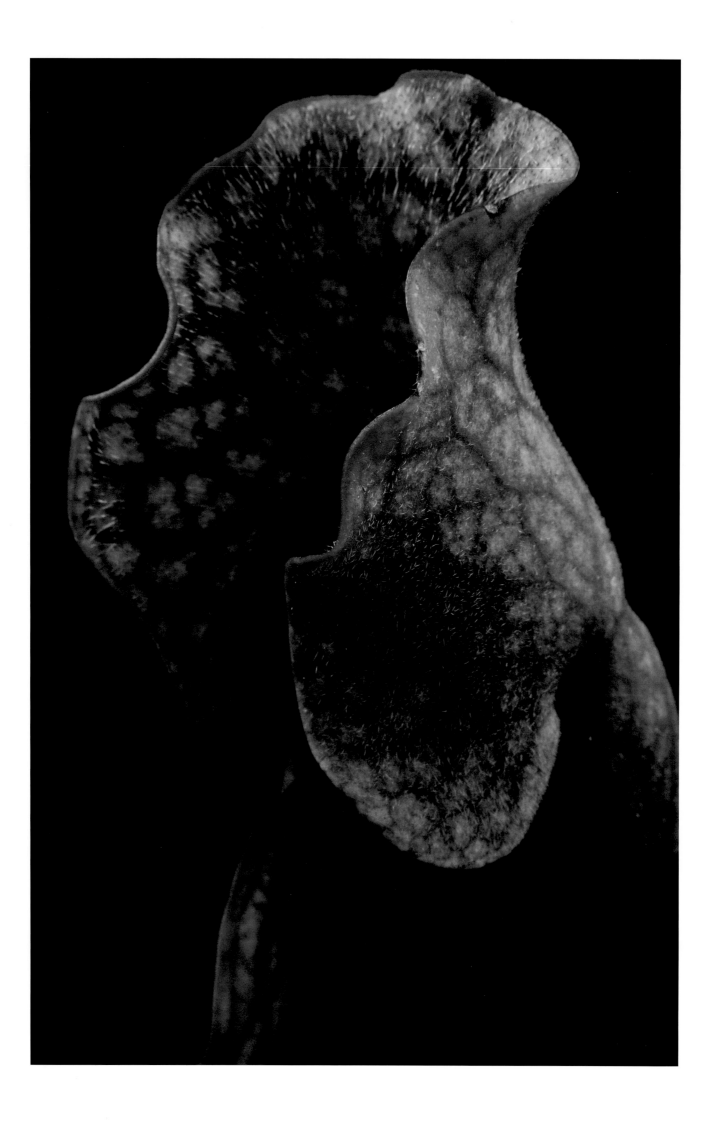

BRUTAL OBSCENE ABOMINATIONS

September 9, 2010

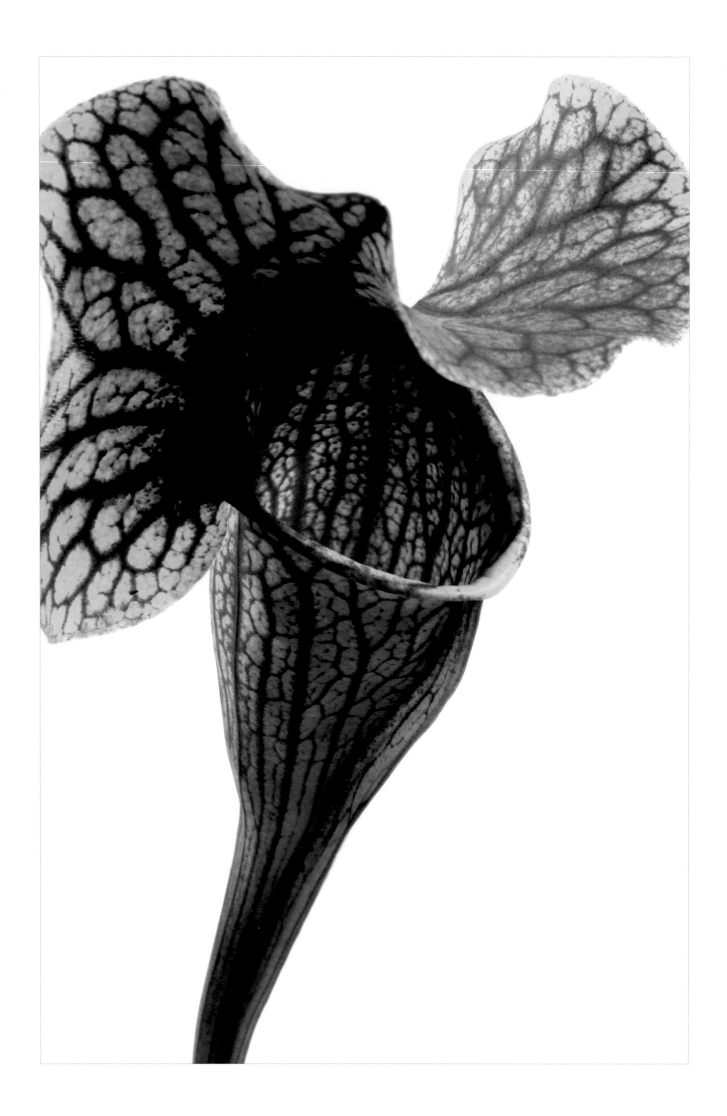

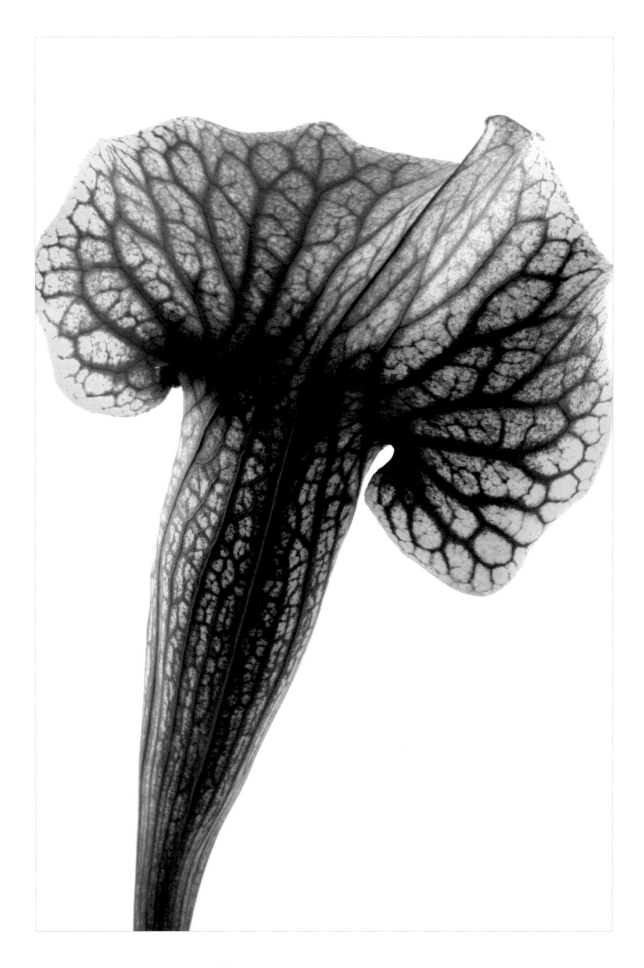

PLATES 23 AND 24

FALSE PROMISES

July 10, 2010

TORCHES OF INSANITY ILLUMINATE US ALL

September 17, 2011

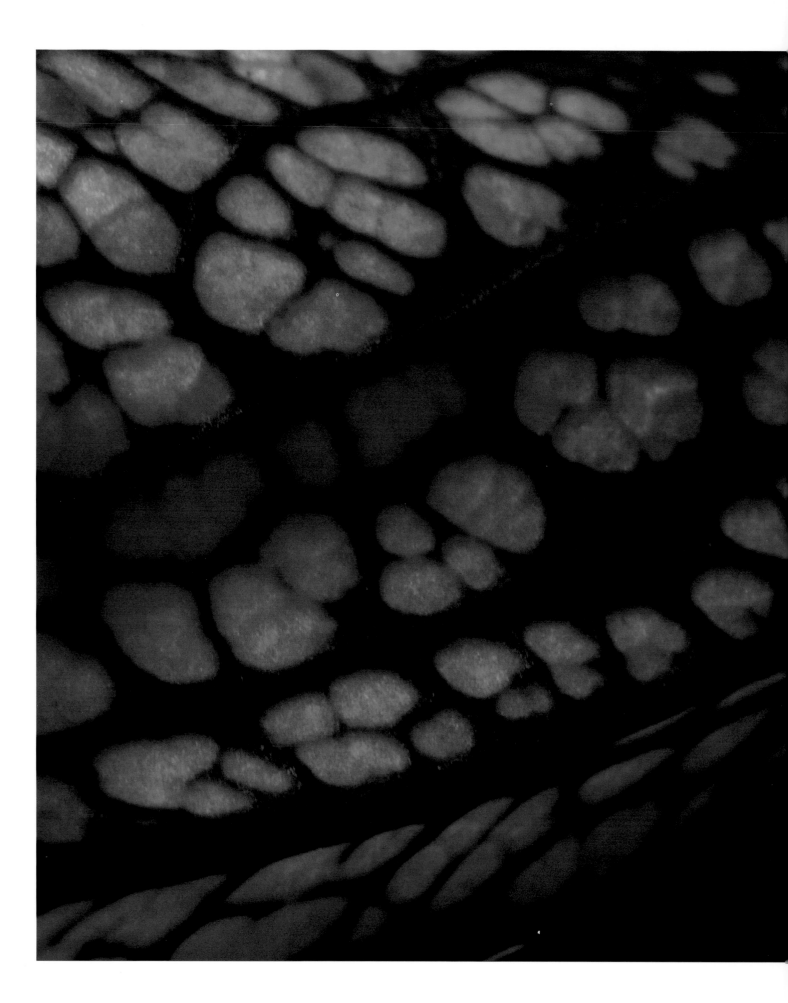

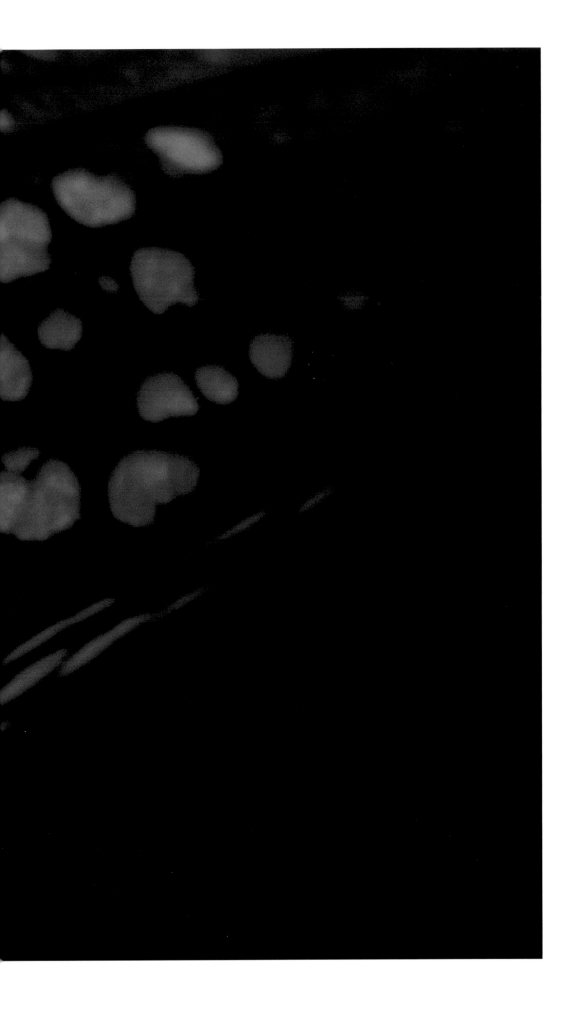

PLATE 27
THRUSTING TURGID
PENETRATION
October 26, 2013

PLATE 28
RAPTURE
September 9, 2010

44

PLATE 29
THROUGH THE EYES OF THE VOYEUR
April 24, 2010

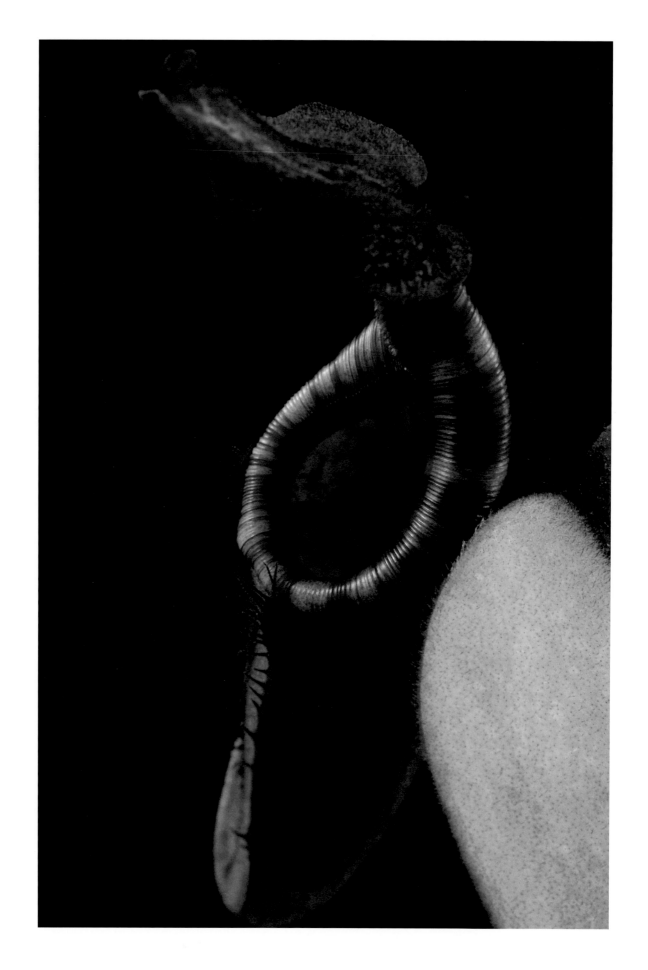

PLATE 30
QUIET LURKING FOR AN EXQUISITE AMBUSH

September 18, 2010

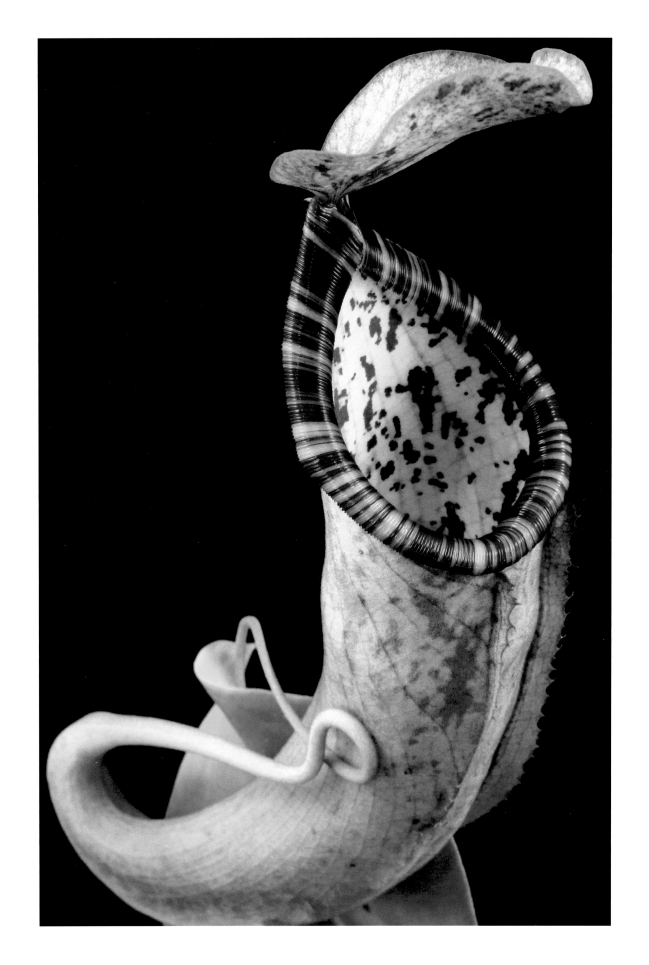

PLATE 31

TWISTED GRACE

September 8, 2010

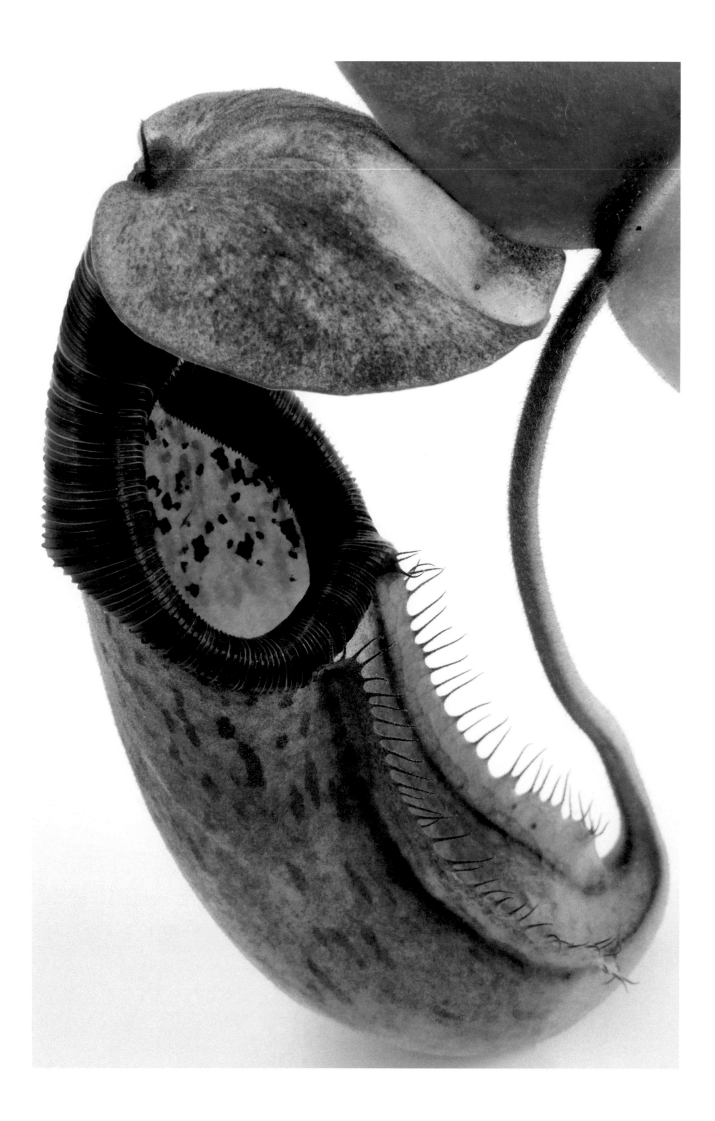

OBSESSIONS OF DEBAUCHERY AND THE LECHEROUS FANTASIES
THAT ACCOMPANY THEM

October 11, 2010

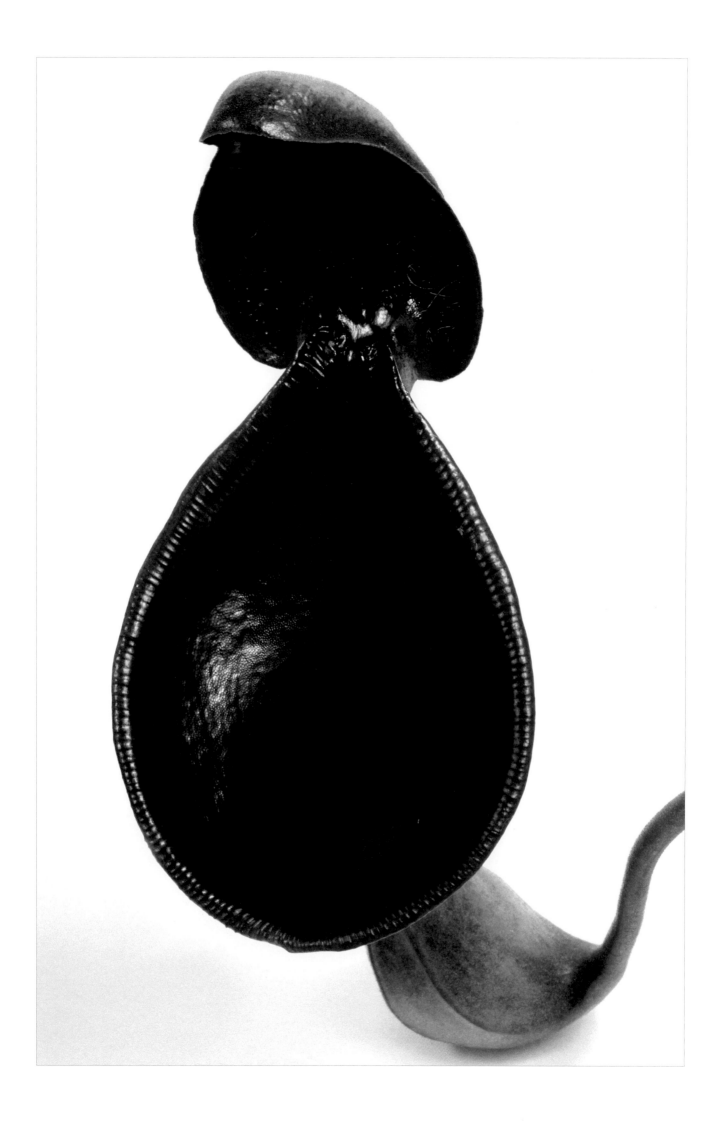

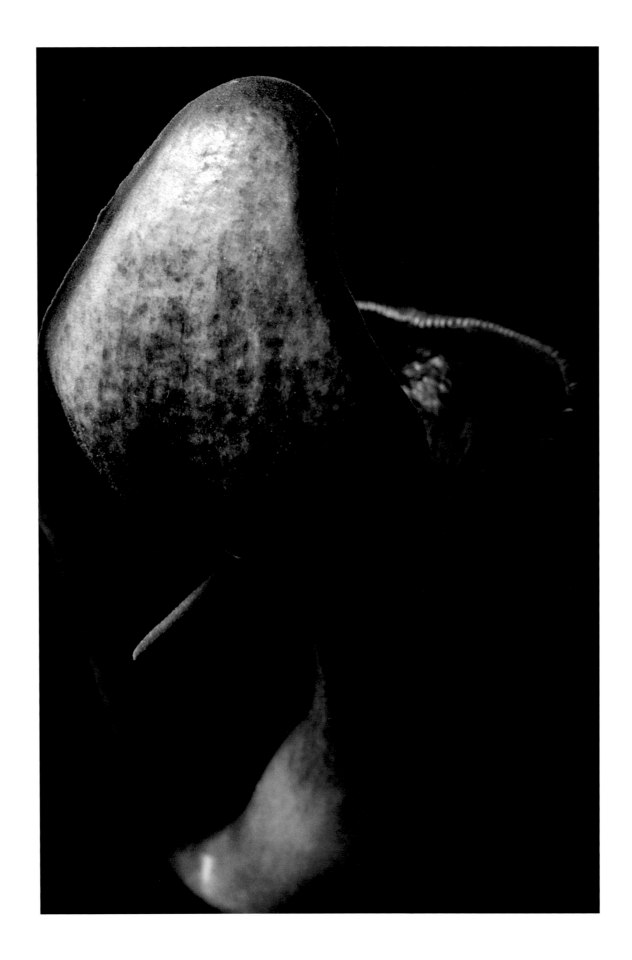

THE BOUNDLESS APPETITE POSSESSED
BY GREED'S GAPING GULLET

April 8, 2012

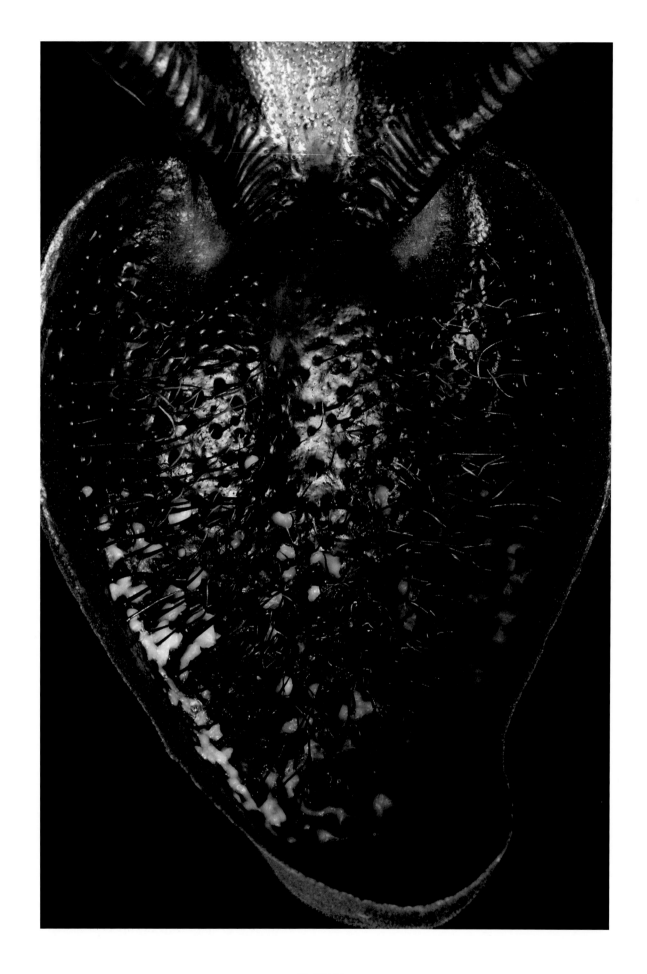

PLATE 36

IMMORAL INDULGENCES TASTE DELICIOUS

April 8, 2012

PLATE 37

SUCCESS THROUGH RUTHLESS EXPLOITATION

September 18, 2010

PLATES 38 AND 39

THE EROTIC NATURE OF FEAR

June 5, 2011

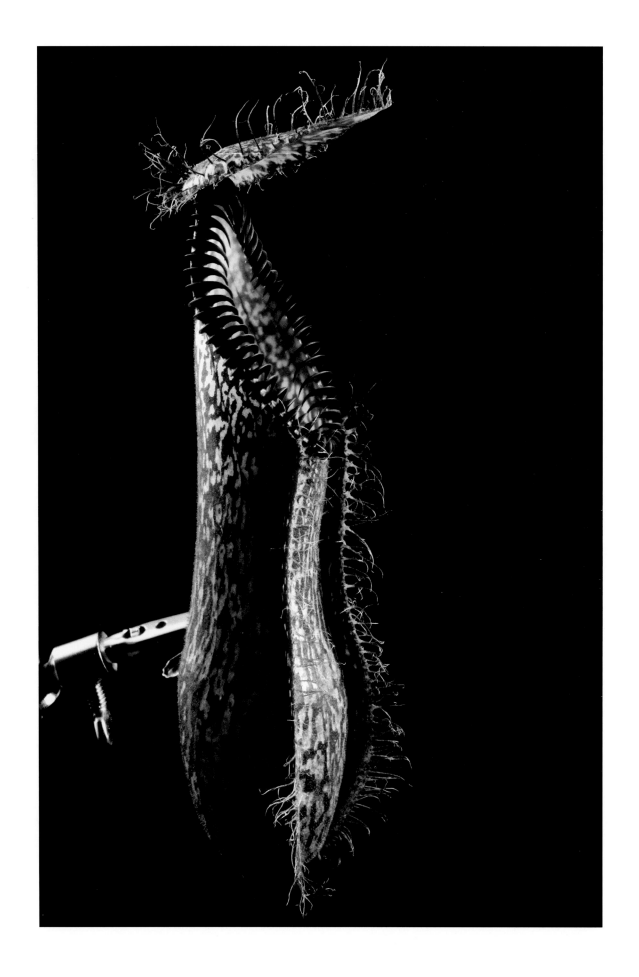

PLATE 40

UNTITLED – *Nepenthes hamata* with photography studio armature

June 5, 2011

PLATE 41

ANARCHY

June 5, 2011

HAUNTING LAMENTATIONS OF BEASTS MOST FOUL

November 26, 2011

PLATES 44 AND 45

HORNS OF WRATH

November 9, 2013

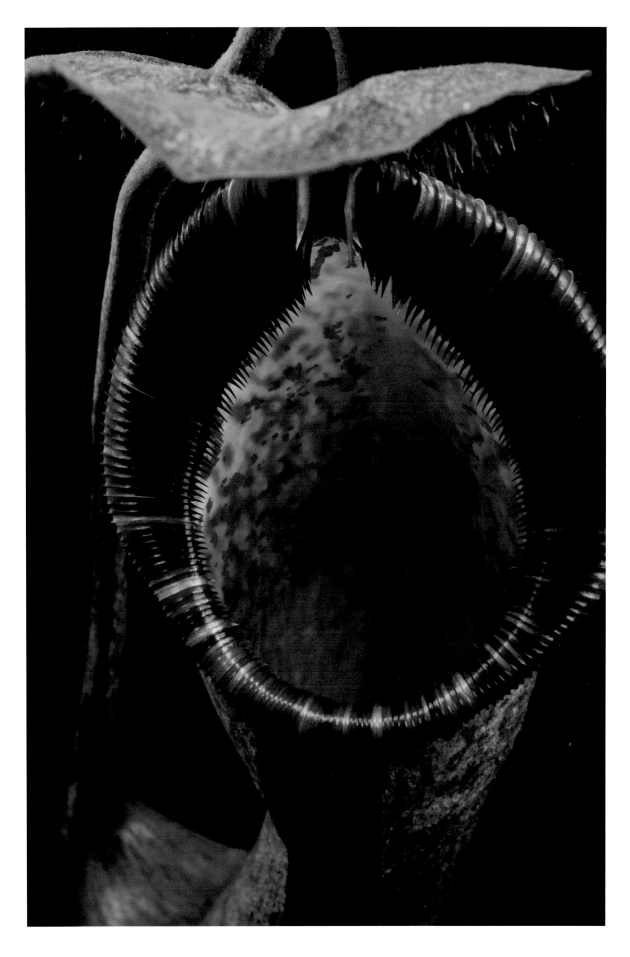

PLATES 46 AND 47

BEAUTIFULLY GROTESQUE

November 9, 2013

PLATE 48
SCOURGE ACROSS THE
PLAINS OF HADES
November 9, 2013

PLATE 49
WHITE HOT FURY
November 10, 2013

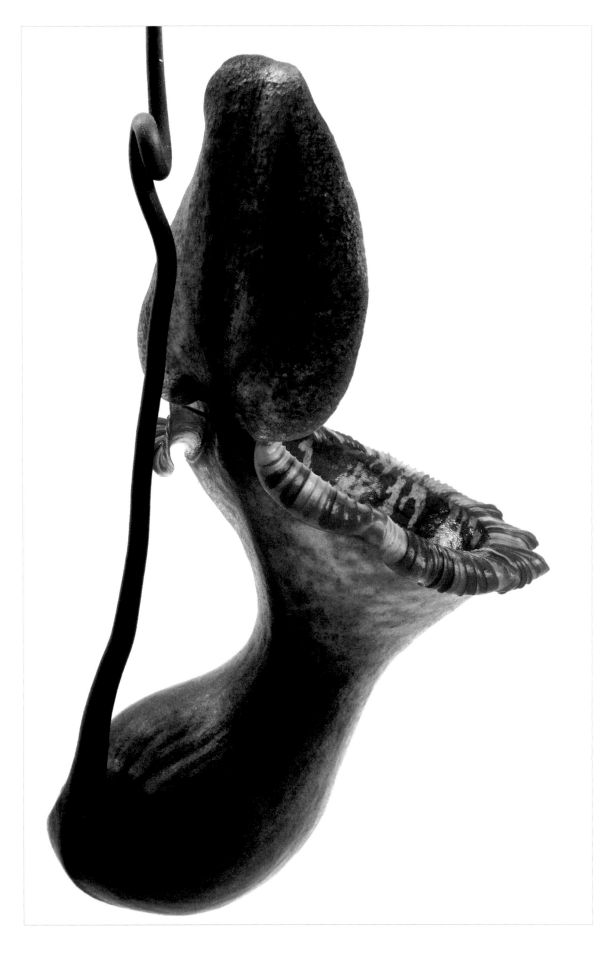

VOLUPTUOUS TEMPTATION IN CARNAL BLISS

May 13, 2012

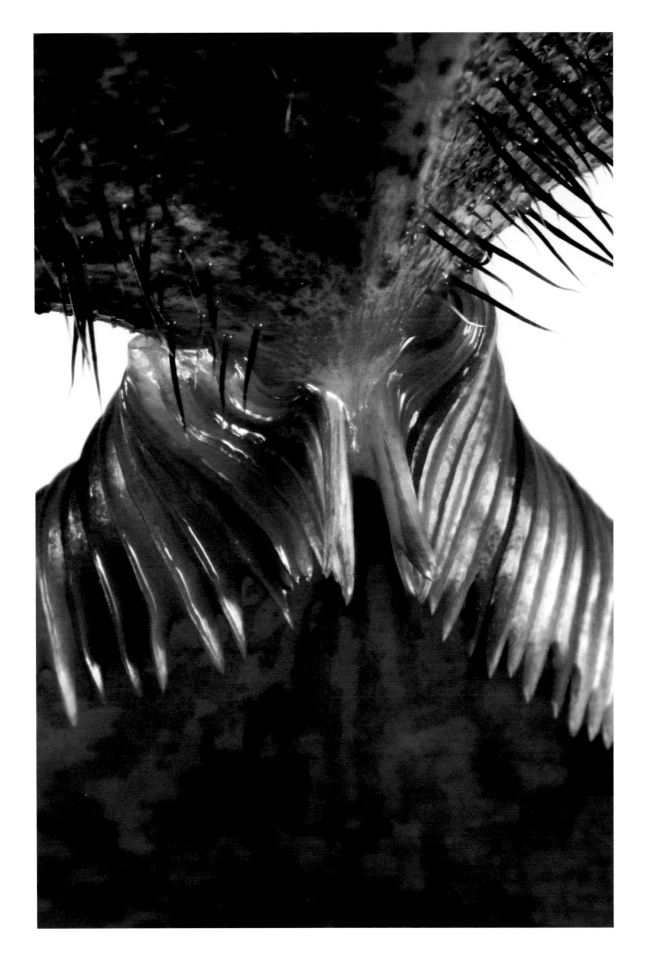

PLATES 52 AND 53

BIRTH OF SOMETHING HORRIBLE

September 29, 2011

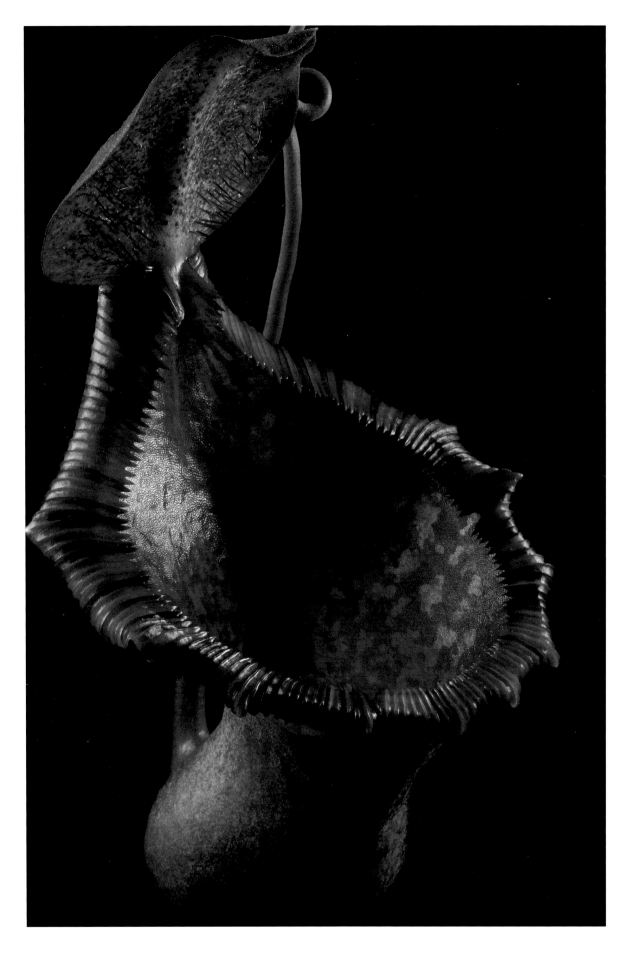

PLATES 54 AND 55
DISTORTED PERVERSIONS
May 3, 2014

PULSING IRRESISTIBLE COMPULSIONS

June 3, 2015

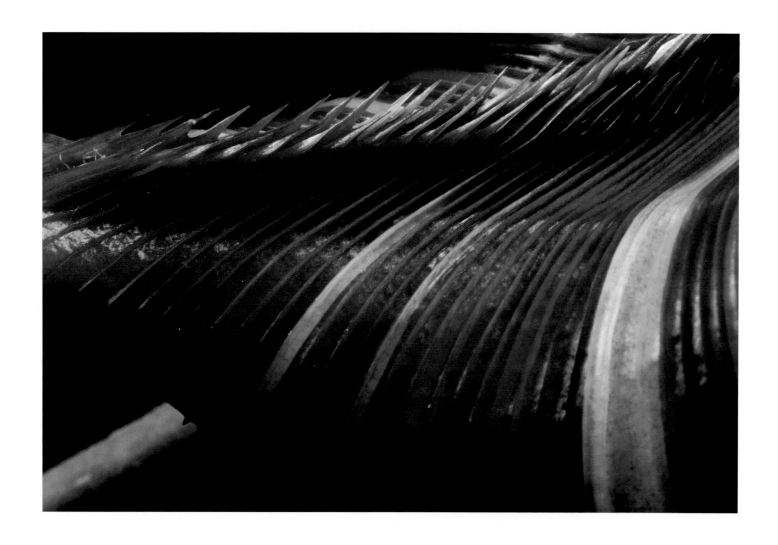

PLATE 58
SURGE
June 1, 2015

PLATE 59
OF UNSPEAKABLE ATROCITIES

June 2, 2015

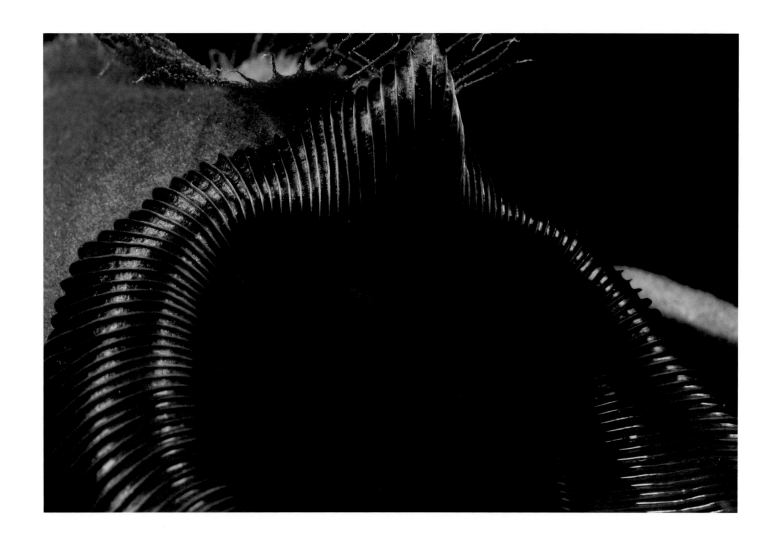

PLATE 60

APPROACH THE WRETCHED HOLLOW

May 25, 2015

PLATE 61

FLOWING LUXURIOUS PAIN

May 28, 2015

PLATE 62
DESTINY MATTERS
LITTLE TO THE DAMNED
May 28, 2015

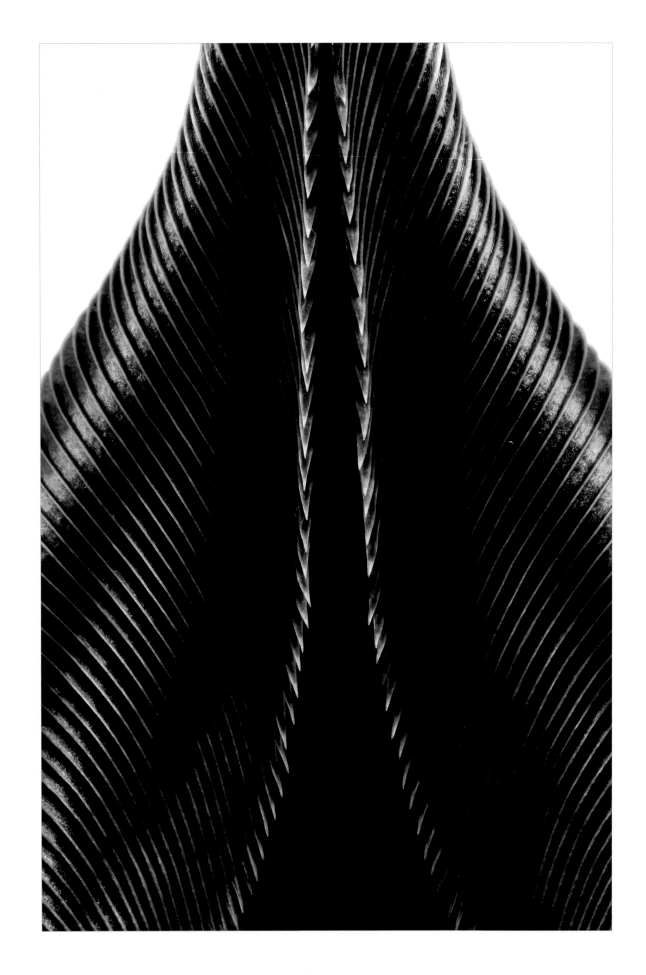

PASSAGE TO FORBIDDEN PLEASURES

May 28, 2015

PLATE 64
RAGGED SLIT
May 26, 2015

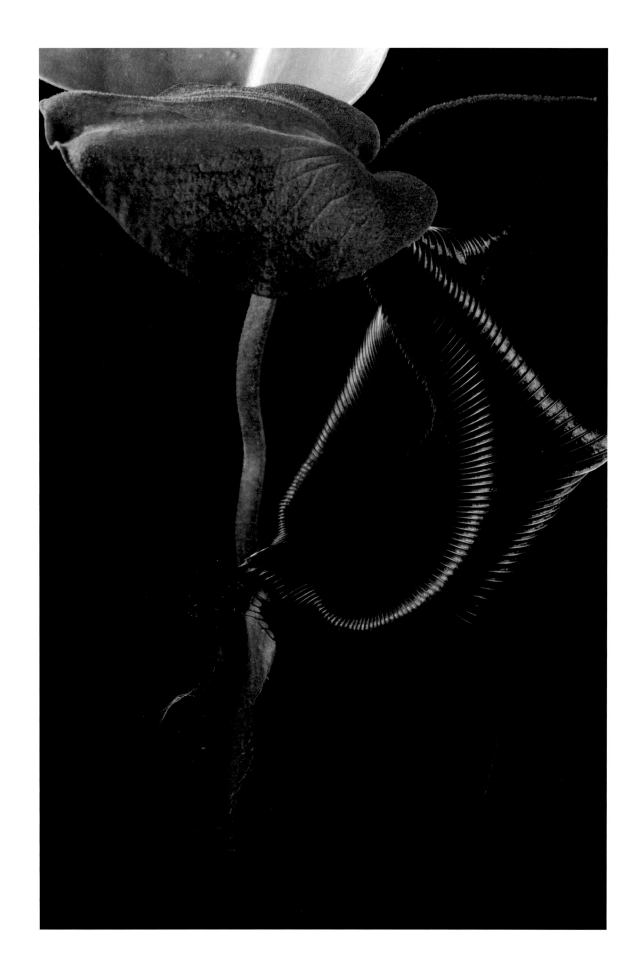

BEWARE THE HIDDEN SACRIFICE IN THE PROMISE OF REWARD

May 25, 2015

CAST INTO THE DELIGHTFUL PITS OF FRENZIED MADNESS

September 3, 2013

PLATE 69

REND

September 3, 2013

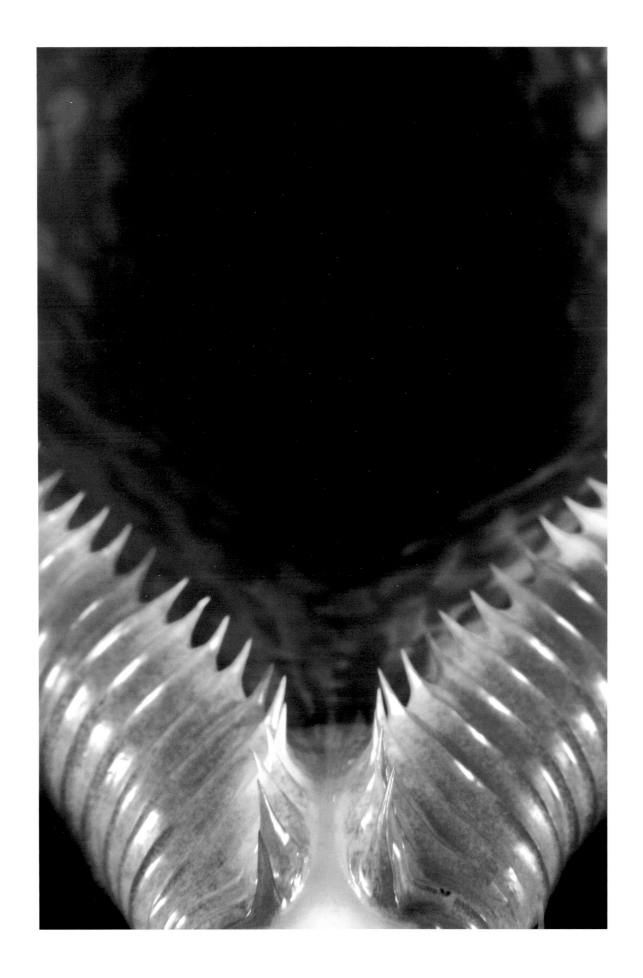

PLATE 70

THE HOLE

July 6, 2015

PLATES 71 AND 72
BUTCHER'S ADORATION
July 6, 2015

PLATE 73
ETHEREAL MACHINATIONS FROM BEYOND THE GRAVE

May 4, 2014

PLATE 74

THE HAZY MIST OF LETHARGY CREEPS

November 8, 2015

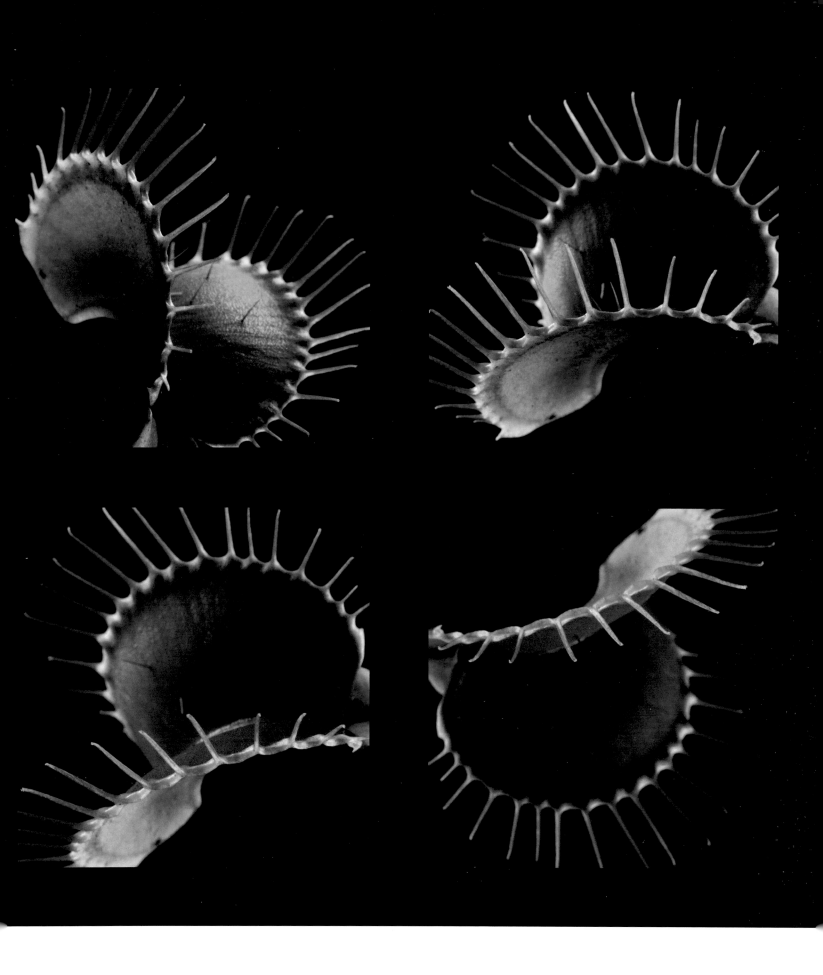

PLATE 75
FLUTTERING MOVEMENTS IN THE ELEGANT DANCE WITH DEATH

September 30, 2012

Cultivation of Carnivorous Plants

The cultivation of carnivorous plants is not just the realm of the lone mad-scientist. There are many throughout the world today who take part in this unconventional and dynamic segment of home gardening. The successful care of these plants can be demanding work but is not insurmountable so long as certain guidelines are followed. Some of the most spectacular and sought-after carnivorous plants can require much more intense effort, which can be difficult to provide, while other plants can be equally as striking and much easier to maintain. Many of these plants are commercially available from a wide selection of retail sources. Some of the most popular ones are found seasonally in the major gardening stores, while the greatest varieties and healthiest specimens are seen at specialty businesses that offer mail-order sales through their websites. Described here are the techniques that I have personally developed over time to fit the needs for the climate where I live, which is on Long Island, NY, the border between the mid-Atlantic and northeast regions of the US. It is often quite hot and humid in the summer and usually cold and snowy in the winter, with the occasional storm—Hurricane Sandy in 2012 was especially disruptive, as I live close to the bays of the southern shoreline. New York's climate presents many challenges as to the care for these plants, and so I grow most of my plants indoors year-round with a few exceptions.

The most important factors to be considered are lighting, water, soil, and temperature. Humidity, while very beneficial when high, does not seem to be as urgent as the other factors. In fact, there have been times during the winter when the humidity levels in my grow areas were as low as around 20 percent for periods of time, although normally the levels are between 45 percent and 75 percent during the growing season. It is best to keep in mind that some plants will not perform well under these low-humidity conditions. I have purposely avoided those plants that require the higher humidity levels in order to keep this project fairly simple and versatile.

Nepenthes robcantleyi in highland grow chamber.
August 26, 2014

For the lighting of the plants that are grown indoors, I use standard T12 and T8 florescent light fixtures with cool-white light bulbs, which are easily attainable and surprisingly effective. It is recommended to replace the bulbs every year even if they are still emitting light because the energy the plants receive from them dwindles over time. The lights are all plugged into automatic timers to switch on or off, with the photoperiods determined according to the types of plants and the time of the year. The tap water from most people's homes is usually unsuitable for carnivorous plants as it normally contains salts and chemicals that, while necessary for safe drinking standards for us humans, will harm and kill these plants over time. I use distilled water from the local supermarket to water the plants. Water from a reverse-osmosis filter or rain water will work just as well, but with rain water, there can be contamination of things living with your plants soon enough, which will dirty up your clean grow area indoors. As for the reverse-osmosis filter, I simply never took the time to set one up where I live, although some units can be fairly easy and trouble-free except for the fact that they produce large quantities of waste water, which could be an issue in places with limited supplies of municipal water.

Perhaps the most important step that I took was to separate the plants into different growing areas to specialize the temperatures for them. For instance, I have two separate grow chambers for the *Nepenthes* tropical pitcher plants, and they are very similar in their layouts, with the major difference being the temperatures maintained for them.

The Lowland Grow Chamber

The *Nepenthes* that grow naturally in the peat forests and swamps in the tropics at the lower elevations, near sea level, require warmer temperatures. I maintain daytime high temperatures warmer than 90°F (32°C) during the summer and above 75°F (24°C) during the winter. The nighttime low temperatures are usually higher than 75°F (24°C) during the summer and at times will dip into the high 60s (15.5°C) for periods of time during the winter. They prefer high amounts of humidity with a well-flushed soil mix that remains moist and also well drained. For this I use Canadian milled *Sphagnum* peat moss that is very well mixed with cedar bark, clay pebbles, pumice rock, and perlite to retain moisture while still facilitating adequate drainage for the soil. The ratio of the soil mix is roughly 40 percent peat moss and 60 percent of the other material. The containers for the plants are ceramic, fiberglass, or standard plastic pots with drainage holes at the bottom to allow the water to flow freely through the soil medium when watered from above.

These plants are grown in what is popularly known as a "lowland grow chamber." The chamber I have constructed is in a room where it remains fairly warm in the winter and can be quite hot in the summer. Here I have developed a simple system for temperature and humidity control.

Three sides of the chamber are surrounded by shower curtains, then there are two layers of insulating bubble wrap before an additional layer of decorative shower curtains to cover them all for aesthetics. The shower curtains hang from a simple PVC frame that is itself hung by large carabiner-style clips, clipped to decorative chains that are attached to hooks used for hanging plants from the ceiling. These hooks screw directly through the plaster board and into the beams of the ceiling and have been sufficient to hold the weight of the frame and curtains over the years. The walls behind the chamber are lined with 1"-thick foam insulate board with two layers of the insulate board placed on the floor underneath the chamber. For the front of the chamber, there is a clear plastic shower curtain hung from the PVC frame that is overlapped by the other shower curtains to keep the warmth and humidity contained while still leaving the interior visible and accessible. Inside the chamber are wire rack shelving systems commonly available in the kitchen or storage sections of hardware stores and at home goods stores. The bottom levels of the racks are raised off the ground with heating mats underneath them. In the center of the bottom of the chamber is a small 5 and a half gallon aquarium with a large 55-gallon aquarium water heater to warm the water to above 80°F (26.7°C), creating additional warmth and humidity during the cold, dry winter months in New York. Plastic bins are placed on the shelves of the rack, then there are platforms arranged in the bins, and the plants are placed on top of these platforms.

The plants are all in freely-draining pots that are individually top watered so that the water drains through them to collect in the plastic bins underneath. The platforms are there to elevate the plants so that they do not sit in the water that collects at the bottom of the bins. When the water levels rise to the platforms, the bins are emptied by using an electric siphon pump. They are also hand-misted with a spray bottle using distilled water every time the plants are watered, which is normally once every three to four days. At first, there were two fixtures of 48" two-bulb T12 florescent lights hanging at the top of the chamber with the plastic bins for the plants on top of a table inside the chamber. Then, as the plants grew larger and the chamber was expanded, the table was removed and replaced with the wire-rack shelving system. That was when a third 48" two-bulb T12 florescent light fixture was set midway down from the top to provide lighting to the lower levels of the chamber. After another rearrangement a couple of years later, there were three fixtures of 48" two-bulb T12 florescent lights hanging at the top of the chamber and two fixtures of 24" two-bulb T12 florescent lights on the lower level of the wire-rack shelving system in the chamber, all of them operating on timers set for the same fourteen-hour photoperiod.

The *Nepenthes* that have been grown in this lowland chamber are: the hybrid *N. × dyeriana, N. hemsleyana,* the cultivar *N.* 'Il de France', *N. merrilliana × truncata, N. maxima* x *veitchii, N.* (*maxima × veitchii*) × *truncata, N. ampullaria, N. ampullaria* 'Cantley's Red', and also the Rainbow plant, *Byblis liniflora.*

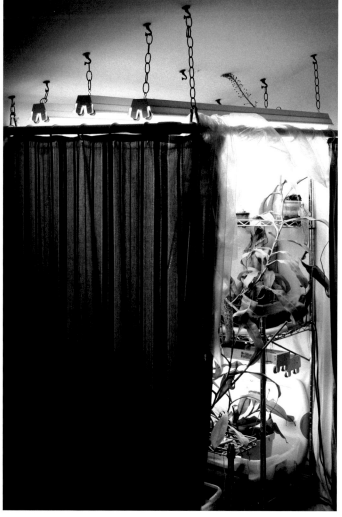

Lowland grow chamber.
September 9, 2010

The Highland Grow Chamber

Alpine-tropical *Nepenthes* grow at the higher elevations on mountains in the tropics and so require cooler temperatures that swing from approximately 75°F (24°C) during the day, to 55°F (12.8°C) at night. Temperatures that are too warm for too long of a time will degrade the plants' health and eventually kill them. They appreciate high amounts of humidity with well-flushed soil that is also well drained.

My preferred soil mix is live New Zealand *Sphagnum* moss with some chunky material mixed in, such as cedar bark, clay pebbles, pumice rock, and perlite to facilitate drainage so that the moss does not condense and become packed too tightly. The ratio for this soil mix is roughly 60 percent live *Sphagnum* moss and 40 percent of the other material. The *Sphagnum* moss the plants grow in spills into the surrounding bins, filling them out where many other interesting plants are grown as well. These associate plants growing in the moss are the carnivorous *Utricularia*

longifolia, U. reniformis, U. calycifida 'Asenath Waite', *U.* 'Jitka'—the cultivar hybrid of *U. quelchii* × *praetermissa,* and also the sundew *Drosera prolifera*. The non-carnivorous plant associates growing in the moss are *Selaginella kraussiana, Episcia* 'Silver Skies', *Ficus pumila var. minima, Ruellia makoyana, Begonia* 'Little Darling', the jewel orchids *Anoectochilus albolineatus* and *Goodyera pusilla*, the orchid *Paphiopedilum* 'Black Jack', and a few unidentified species of *Tillandsia*. All of the *Nepenthes* are grown in mesh pots or larger mesh trays for additional drainage and air movement to the roots. The plants that require these conditions are grown in what is popularly known as a "highland grow chamber." I have constructed the highland grow chamber in my kitchen pantry in a downstairs area of the home that is less heated in the winter and air-conditioned 24/7 in the summertime, staying fairly cool year-round. The temperatures during the summer are normally no higher than 78°F (25.6°C) with lows of generally 65°F (18.3°C).

Highland grow chamber.
August 26, 2014

During the winter, the low temperatures have gotten as low as 44°F (6.7°C), but normally are no less than 50°F (10°C) with highs rarely reaching above 65°F (18.3°C). While perhaps not being completely ideal, this has served me well over the years, and the plants have flourished with great health, the mature ones flowering at regular times every year.

The chamber itself follows a principle very similar to the lowland grow chamber, in that it is made using standard wire rack shelving systems with plastic bins placed on the shelves, and the potted plants resting on platforms in the bins. In this case, the racks are placed inside my kitchen pantry, which gives them a fairly open area that is still well protected. The plants are individually top watered in the same manner as the lowland *Nepenthes* so that the water drains through the potted plants to collect in the plastic bins underneath, and the bins are emptied by a siphon pump as needed. The plants are also hand-misted with a spray bottle using distilled water every time the plants are watered, which is normally once every three to four days, again the same as the plants in the lowland grow chamber.

Four fixtures of 48" two-bulb T12 florescent lights hang at the top of the racks and are on a fourteen-hour photoperiod. To increase the humidity of the chamber, I have used a three-disc ultrasonic fogger placed in a round plastic food container filled with distilled water. The plants do seem to appreciate this, although the system does take up a good amount of the available growing space in the chamber. Underneath, a section of the rack system is used for food and drink storage, as it is in the kitchen pantry after all.

I have grown many highland *Nepenthes* in this chamber. Sometimes when older plants grew too large, I sold or traded them to make way for newer plants, especially when newly created hybrids became available. Some of the *Nepenthes* that I have grown in this chamber are: the cultivar *N.* 'The Succubus', the cultivar *N.* 'H.R. Giger', a female *N. lowii*, *N. lowii × veitchii*, *N. lowii × truncata*, *N. truncata × ephippiata*, *N. hamata*, *N. truncata × hamata*, *N. × trusmadiensis*, *N. ventricosa × alata*, *N. ventricosa*, *N. ventricosa × (× trusmadiensis)*, the cultivar *N.* 'Lady Pauline'—hybrid between *N. talangensis* and *N. maxima*, *N. eymae × (stenophylla × lowii)*, and *N. robcantleyi*.

For all of the *Nepenthes* in both the lowland grow chamber and the highland grow chamber, I use a diluted solution of Maxsea Seaweed fertilizer 16-16-16 about once a month, which can have great benefits for the indoor-grown *Nepenthes* that do not have the same opportunities for capturing prey as those grown outdoors in the tropics.

Highland grow chamber.
December 4, 2014

Fish Tank Terrariums

For carnivorous plant cultivation, the classic aquarium, or fish tank, terrarium is a much simpler arrangement. In my case, it is a 75-gallon aquarium turned onto its side so that its open top is at the front to enable generous ventilation and air movement. A small plug-in fan blows across and slightly away from the open front of the terrarium to further aid the air circulation. This air circulation is very important for the aquarium terrarium, as fungus can develop in a confined and humid area with stagnant air; fungus can be very damaging to the plants and difficult to eradicate. The *Nepenthes* grow chambers mentioned earlier are much larger and more open, and so have adequate natural air movement to prevent these problems. The plants that I grow in the fish tank terrarium are temperature-sensitive, cool-growing mountain and coastal plants. These are a varied collection of plants from around the world that grow in cooler areas that are not as wet as the alpine tropicals. They would not tolerate being exposed to the heat of the Long Island summer, nor the frozen winter, and so remain protected indoors year-round.

The fish-tank terrarium is in the same room as the highland grow chamber to keep it cool throughout the year, with the air-conditioner being used in the summer from the middle of June to around the middle of September. Examples of some of the plants that I have grown long-term in this manner are: *Cephalotus follicularis, Darlingtonia californica, Drosera regia, D. binata* 'Marston Dragon', *D. capensis, D. adelae, Byblis liniflora, Pinguicula reticulata, P. cyclosecta, P. moranensis,* and the terrestrial *Utricularia U. sandersonii* and *U. livida,* as well as many others.

These plants are all in ceramic or plastic pots with drainage holes at their bottoms, and are mostly placed in individual water trays. They are watered by pouring the water into the trays before the tray becomes empty; the soil is never allowed to become dry. The exception is *Cephalotus follicularis,* which are best watered through the top once every three to four days, letting the water freely drain out of the bottom. The soil mixture normally used for all of these plants is roughly half Canadian milled *Sphagnum* peat moss and half course sand; I usually use the sand that is sold for pool filters. This is a good standard-type soil mix that I find works great with most carnivorous plants grown in this way. I completely avoid any soil media with any growth aids or nutrients such as Miracle Grow; they are very detrimental for carnivorous plants because the plants are sensitive to those types of products.

Three fixtures of 48" two-bulb T8 florescent lights are placed on top of the tank and a reflective covering called panda film (black on one side; white on the other) is placed on three sides of the tank with the white side facing the inside to increase the lighting for the plants. The low point of the photoperiod in the winter is twelve hours and the high point at the peak of summer is sixteen hours, gradually transitioning from one to the other throughout the year.

Aquarium terrarium.
June 23, 2008

The Maui Orchidarium

There are also ready-made chambers made by Orchidarium and distributed by Dragon Agro Products. I have the triple-lamp unit of the Maui model; it is a specialized vivarium designed for growing orchids that can also be used for growing carnivorous plants with great success, although they unfortunately seem to be discontinued at this time. The Maui Orchidarium is a clear acrylic container topped with three light fixtures of 39-watt biaxial florescent lights under a reflective hood. Built into the top of the light fixture is a vent with a muffin fan blowing out from the inside to assist in air movement and to discharge the warm air that can build up inside the chamber. An acrylic panel separates the lights from the chamber to prevent the lights from drying out the grow area. There is a basin at the bottom to collect excess water and mesh plates to keep the plants elevated and from sitting in the water, which is very helpful for *Nepenthes*. Although somewhat expensive, this is a very effective unit for growing carnivorous plants. Vining *Nepenthes* and the taller species of *Sarracenia* will quickly outgrow the area, so smaller to medium-sized and more compact plants are best used with this system. Over time I have used the Maui for a fairly wide variety of carnivorous plants with great results. The lights are built directly into the chamber and are then plugged into an automatic timer on a photoperiod just as those for the other grow areas. These are very sleek and attractive units that fit well in a room setting and are very nicely designed.

Altogether, there have been much more sophisticated and elaborate systems that have been constructed for growing carnivorous plants. I chose to keep my project simple, effective, fairly inexpensive, and most importantly; manageable. I find it is best to grow the plants in a fashion that is not too demanding and can be sustained over time. The results speak for themselves over the long term. The cultivation of these plants has been a challenge at times, but also has been very rewarding. They have successfully grown and flourished around my home for well over a decade and will continue doing so for many more years to come.

Orchidarium.
December 18, 2005

Nepenthes lowii in the small blue ceramic pot in the center is the same large, flowering plant seen in the photograph on page 101.
The orange ceramic pot to its right is N. × *dyeriana*, which is the large plant in the photograph on page 99.

Outdoor Plants

There are also many different carnivorous plants that can be grown outdoors in the yard. Temperate plants grow in areas of the world that have hot summers and cold winters and so are adapted to go dormant during the cold months of the year. They include carnivorous plants that are native to the eastern Atlantic coast of the US, and these in particular are easy to grow outdoors in the summer on Long Island, New York. During the growing season, the plants are simply placed in a spot in the backyard that is sunny for most of the day with at least four or more hours of direct sunlight. I prefer to expose them to direct sunlight throughout the morning to the early afternoon, with bright shade during the mid-day and exposure to direct sunlight again at the end of the day. This will bring out great coloration without exhausting the plants, for it is possible to sometimes give them too much sun, depending on the circumstances. It is best to observe them daily for a time, after moving them to a new spot, to look for any signs of distress.

Fountain of Tears: Carnivorous plants grown outdoors.
August 24, 2013

Drosera × californica, hybrid of *Drosera filiformis × tracyi.*
August 3, 2013

When the growing season ends, and they begin to go dormant, it is very important to keep the plants protected from the worst of New York's cold winters. For this I use an unheated greenhouse, but large plastic bins covered with lids will work quite well. It is very important to keep them consistently watered throughout their dormant period to prevent their soil from drying out. The freezing temperatures they will experience can break ceramic pottery and so plastic or fiberglass pots are usually best used for plants that are grown outside year-round.

Freezing can also be very harmful to some of the more sensitive of the temperate carnivorous plants, especially the plants from the far southern US that are best not to be exposed to the northern winters. For those, I bring the plants inside for their dormancy and keep them in a place where it is cold, but never freezes. They are set under T12 lights for short photoperiods of around eight hours a day. A proper dormancy is necessary for the long-term health of the temperate plants and should always be respected. As I am in the northeast of the US, I tend to put the plants outside sometime in April or whenever it looks like there will be no more hard frosts, and I bring them back in before the end of October or even the beginning of November, before any hard frosts begin. These temperate carnivorous plants are planted in containers with drainage holes at the bottom and placed in water trays that keep the soil moist at all times. Since the plants are grown outside, most of the time the rain simply waters them, and I also have a container to catch rainwater to supplement that. During dry spells when there is no rain, store-bought distilled water or another alternative source of pure water is used to keep the plants from drying out.

For outdoor temperate plants, the soil mixture I use is the standard mix that is roughly half Canadian milled *Sphagnum* peat moss and half course sand. The plants that I have grown outdoors or in the greenhouse include pitcher plants from the US such as: *Sarracenia purpurea, S. leucophylla, S. minor, S. alata,* and the natural hybrid of *S. flava* and *S. purpurea* known as *S. × catesbaei*. I have also grown temperate sundews such as: *Drosera filiformis, D. tracyi, D. rotundifolia, D. intermedia,* the sundew hybrids *D. × hybrida–D. filiformis × intermedia, D. × belezeana–D. rotundifolia × intermedia, D. × californica–D. filiformis × tracyi,* and *D. × tokaiensis–D. spatulata x rotundifolia,* and also the temperate butterworts *Pinguicula lutea* and *P. planifolia*. And finally, the most well-known and popular of the carnivorous plants, *Dionaea muscipula,* more commonly known as the Venus flytrap. There are also a few non-carnivorous bog plants that I grow alongside them as associates, such as the club-moss *Lycopodium appressum,* the bog orchid *Calopogon tuberosus,* the bog violet *Viola lanceolata,* and cranberry *Vaccinium macrocarpon*.

Protecting Plants from Pests and Disease

Even though carnivorous plants are best known for preying on insects, there are occasional threats from pests and diseases that can be very harmful or fatal to the plants if not properly treated. I fortunately have only had to deal with a few of these nuisances.

Aphids are probably the most commonly encountered trouble, and some carnivorous plants have built-in defenses for these pests such as wooly or bristling textures around the base where their new growth emerges. This is the area these insects normally prefer to feed upon and is the most vulnerable to their predations. Other carnivorous plants do not have such defenses and I find that they can be particularly damaging to Venus flytraps and cape sundews.

My favored treatment is Bonide's Systemic Insect Control, which the plant absorbs into its body enabling the insecticide to continue working after the application. I tend to reapply it once every three or four days for as long as the problem persists.

Spider mites are an especially repugnant bane. Insecticides are of little use as these foul beasties are arachnids and are instead related to spiders and crabs. Liquid Ladybug or Garden Safe's Fungicide3 insect, mite, and fungus control can be helpful, but the best thing to do is to remove the leaves that are infected at once to try to keep the mites from spreading to any other plants.

If all of the leaves need to be removed from the plant to get rid of these tenacious pests, then so be it; new leaves will grow again in time. It is also recommended to rinse off and repot the affected plant into fresh media after trimming all the leaves. The Botrytis fungus (also called gray mold) is a very damaging threat and will ultimately kill the plants it infects. This particularly affects *Cephalotus follicularis* in the winter, if the soil becomes too wet and the air too still. This is perhaps the most difficult problem, and I have found Bonide's Sulpher Fungicide to be helpful but not a complete cure. The only times I have truly eradicated the fungus is when I have placed the plants outside for a few weeks in the spring, or the fall, when it is not too hot outside for the affected plants. The strong, direct sunlight and the exposure to the open air kills off the persistent fungus. Afterwards, I normally repot them with new soil, and the problem is usually solved. In the end, it is best to prevent the Botrytis fungus from occurring in the first place by providing good air circulation.

Carnivorous plants can be sensitive to such pest and disease products, but the ones listed I have found to be safe enough. Overall, these are what I use and although there certainly could be more effective treatments out there, these have been readily available to me and have worked well over the years.

Exhibition of Carnivorous Plants

The exhibition of carnivorous plants is an engaging way for cultivators to introduce the public to this interesting world. Creating artistically designed displays of these living plants will bring a greater visual impact and provide more enjoyment for the viewers as well.

For exhibitions, glazed ceramic pottery can be used as containers to give a bonsai aesthetic to carnivorous plants. This is by no means uncommonly done by carnivorous plant cultivators, and the types of ceramic pots that are recommended for use are the ones that already have sizable drainage holes at the bottom of them. Pottery for orchids normally works well, and sometimes pots for bonsai. The bonsai pottery is usually quite shallow and so should only be used for plants that do not need as deep a container for their roots, such as *Utricularia, Pinguicula*, pygmy *Drosera,* and other smaller *Drosera.* If a desired ceramic pot is found, but it does not have drainage holes in the bottom, a hole can be chiseled into the bottom, but this is fairly difficult to do and the pottery can easily crumble if one is not careful when doing so. The end results tend to look a bit ragged and are rough,

but the goal is just to have a drainage hole, and since it is on the bottom, it does not need to look especially presentable.

Once the plant is potted into the decorative ceramic pottery with its appropriate soil mix, pinches of various types of mosses can be added to the corners of the soil surface that will spread and fill as a top-dressing, giving the subject a further bonsai aesthetic. It is best to keep in mind that these mosses can overwhelm smaller carnivorous plants, so they should only be used with medium- to larger-sized plants. Sometimes terrestrial *Utricularia* can be added as well, or they just seem to migrate on their own if they are already part of the collection; they are always an attractive addition to the top dressing, especially when they go into flower.

The final touch is to trim and clean the plants for the exhibition. While it is advisable to cut the dead and unsightly growth, sometimes it is better to leave some of this untouched. For example, if only the most perfect growth is left, one can end up with a *Nepenthes* that is a long stalk with few leaves and only one or two pitchers on it. It is the author's opinion that it is best to trim and

Nepenthes 'The Succubus' Cultivar.
Display at the International Carnivorous Plant Society 2012 Conference.
August 14, 2012

Nepenthes 'H. R. Giger' cultivar.
Display at Bay Port Flower Houses.
March 24, 2013

shape the plant according to how it has grown naturally, working with the flow and direction that the plant has decided upon. Then, leave some dead or dying material while trimming the rest of the plant in a manner that leaves it looking full, healthy, and showing the progression of its growth. This will give the displayed plant a look that is natural, sensible, and balanced, and every element will belong exactly where it is. Sometimes even unintended weeds that grow in the pots can be used as complimentary associates if they are properly groomed.

Planted globe terrariums of the fishbowl type can be very problematic for most carnivorous plants for long-term cultivation. The main problem with these types of terrariums is that there is no drainage and so the water tends to get stagnant and the soil becomes waterlogged and mucky. Because the terrariums are fairly well enclosed in glass, there is little air movement or ventilation. *Sarracenia* will survive, although their growth dramatically improves after transplanting them back to drained containers. *Dionaea*, *Drosera*, *Pinguicula*, and especially *Nepenthes* are all completely unsuitable for this style of planting and will languish and decline even under the best conditions.

There is an exception to the rule for the unsuitability of glass globe terrariums, and that is for the terrestrial *Utricularia*. These plants will flourish and enjoy these undrained conditions, periodically sending up masses of their exquisite little flowers, making for very attractive arrangements. There is still room for experimentation and for new techniques to be developed, but for a standard planting, the glass-globe terrariums are one of the least ideal ways to grow carnivorous plants for the long-term, and growers should be aware of these limitations.

For a number of public exhibitions, I have created temporary *Nepenthes* displays that were purely aesthetic forms arranged with various types of associate plants that would not normally grow together in the wild. The centerpieces were the *Nepenthes*, which are usually man-made horticultural hybrids. The materials used for these displays include: plastic containers, various forms of driftwood, polished river stones, *Sphagnum* moss, associate plants, and the *Nepenthes* themselves. The types of driftwood that are used are sanded manzanita branches and sanded ghostwood, and sometimes other types of rot-resistant wood. The pieces of driftwood are arranged before selecting where the

Nepenthes will be placed. The placement of the large pieces of driftwood represent the movement of the wind through the form, giving it direction and life. Once the *Nepenthes* have been placed, their pots are set into plastic food containers to capture whatever water drains through the *Nepenthes* when they are watered after the display is finished. Once the *Nepenthes* and the large driftwood are arranged, the rest of the form will begin to take shape. All voids in between the parts of the display that will be later covered and hidden are filled with lighter materials such as dried *Sphagnum* moss and the same clay pebbles that are used for potting mixes. Then, black polished river stones are piled around the base so that they gently slope outward from the containers that the *Nepenthes* are housed in. The river stones are arranged to create shapes that appear to flow from the base, as water would, to represent the flow of water through the form. Next, carpets of live *Sphagnum* moss and *Selaginella* are draped over the topmost parts of the stone piles at the bases of the *Nepenthes*, fully concealing any of the supporting understructure. Then, associate plants selected from the plants that are grown in the moss of the highland grow chamber are artistically arranged in the live *Sphagnum* moss and *Selaginella*. This represents the earth, growing up from the base and giving the form mass and continuing the movement of the wind and the water.

The *Nepenthes* are the centerpiece of the display, and so are at the center of attention. They are arranged to synchronize with the form of the display so that they appear to emerge and grow from this idealized, sculptured landscape. Overall, the design is meant to evoke the flow of movement and elements. Although the display may appear to be quite naturalistic to the viewer, these displays are not meant to be habitat representations. My displays are experimental aesthetic pieces and are simply meant to be enjoyed for their beauty and grace as works of naturalistic art. Many design elements have influenced the displays that I have created. There is the elegance and use of space in Japanese courtyard gardens, the use of form and voids in Zen rock gardens, the windswept green landscapes surrounding the European stone megaliths, the natural material and delicate construction of fairy gardens, the artistic craft of glass-globe terrariums, the luxurious tropical presentations in orchid displays, and of course the sculptured, natural aesthetics of bonsai.

Carnivorous plants are still an emerging class in modern horticulture, often presented to the public as carnival-like curiosities and relegated to the sidelines in the world of serious cultivation for ornamental plants. They were once held in the highest esteem from their first discoveries during the Age of Enlightenment to the Victorian era, and they are well poised to do so again once public consciousness moves beyond the novelty of their habits and carnivorous plants become appreciated for the truly unique and beautiful foliage they possess.

Combination of various highland *Nepenthes*.
Display at the South Fork Natural History Museum.
October 13, 2013

Dionaea muscipula in flower.
June 13, 2008

Dionaea muscipula with emerging flower stalks.
April 30, 2008

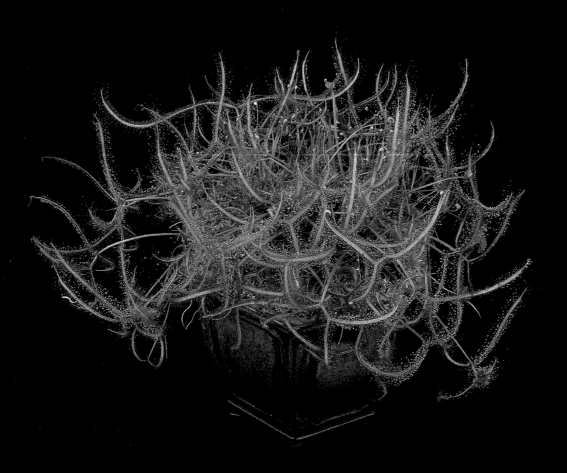

Drosera binata 'Marston Dragon' cultivar.
July 13, 2009

Drosera regia.
May 15, 2009

Drosera regia 'Big Easy' cultivar.
January 2, 2009

Byblis liniflora,
also known as the rainbow plant.
It is found in Australia,
Indonesia and Papua New Guinea
in seasonally wet sands in bogs
and marshes.
It is listed as a species of
Least Concern
on the IUCN Red List.
September 16, 2007

Combination planting of
Pinguicula moranensis,
P. cyclosecta,
Byblis liniflora,
and
Pinguicula laueana, which is a
butterwort from the
Mexican state of Oaxaca
and has not been evaluated by the
IUCN at this time.
November 23, 2008

Cephalotus follicularis.
July 11, 2009

Cephalotus follicularis.
July 11, 2009

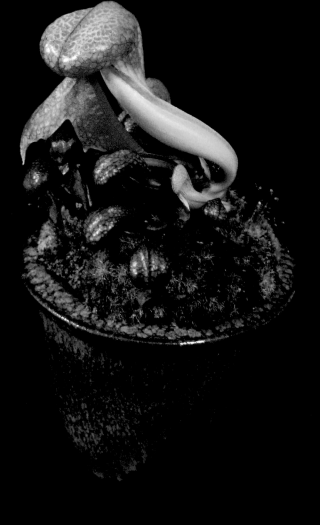

Darlingtonia californica.
June 23, 2008

Sarracenia purpurea subsp. *venosa*
with unusually short flower stalk.
November 23, 2008

Sarracenia x *catesbaei*.
November 23, 2008

Nepenthes 'The Succubus' cultivar.
February 28, 2008

Nepenthes hamata.
July 11, 2009

Nepenthes maxima × *veitchii*
is a man–made hybrid of *N. maxima,* which is from
New Guinea, Sulawesi, and the Malaku Islands,
crossed with *N. veitchii,* which is endemic to
the island of Borneo.
May 15, 2009

Nepenthes maxima × *veitchii.*
May 11, 2009

Nepenthes ventricosa × *alata*
is a hybrid of *N. ventricosa,* which is endemic
to the Philippines, crossed with *N. alata,*
which is endemic to the Philippines as well.
June 23, 2008

Nepenthes ventricosa
is endemic to the Philippines from the islands
of Luzon, Panay, and Sibuyan, growing at
an elevation between 3,280 feet (1000 m)
and 6,650 feet (2000 m) above sea level.
It is listed as Near Threatened on the
IUCN Red List.
April 30, 2008

Native Carnivorous Plants

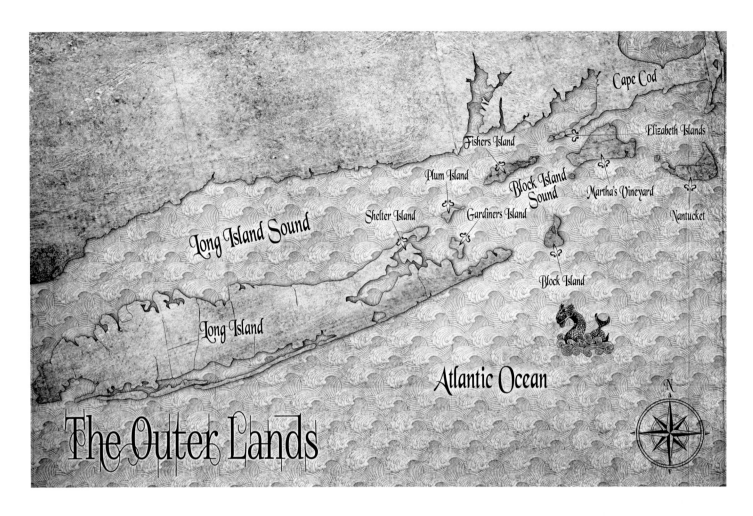

The Outer Lands. Note: Not to scale.
Credit: Joel Koos

Twenty thousand years ago, the glaciers that had covered the northeast of the United States were gradually melting away, pulsing with retreats and advances over the thousands of years at the end of this age of ice. While diminishing, they deposited massive amounts of boulders, loose rock, and gravel with sandy outwash plains fanning out from these jumbled heaps to form the northeastern terminal moraine archipelagic region that is known today as "The Outer Lands."

While this was occurring, sea levels began to rise as the waters locked up in the glaciers were released, surrounding and isolating what became the islands of the Outer Lands. The major components of this archipelago include Long Island, Shelter Island, Gardiners Island, Plum Island, Fishers Island, Block Island, the Elizabeth Islands, the islands of Nantucket and Martha's Vineyard, and the peninsula of Cape Cod.

The Outer Lands are also the northernmost part of the physiographic region of the Atlantic Coastal Plain. This region continues south, along the rest of the Atlantic seaboard extending across to the panhandle of Florida on the Gulf Coast and is characterized by low-lying and level landscapes filled with rivers, swamps, marshes, and other wetlands.

Long Island, New York, is the largest island of this archipelago, and the largest in the continental United States as well. Across this island there are many ideal and varied habitats for carnivorous plants, of which there are sixteen native species in three genera. These habitats include familiar places where carnivorous plants are known to grow, such as in the *Sphagnum* moss along pristine river banks, or within wet, sunny meadows deep in the forest. But the most spectacular habitats can be found in some rather surprising locations. Great dunes of sand approaching forty feet (12.2 meters) in height shift with the winds and slowly move across the landscape to bury even trees in their path. Within these dunes are swaths that dip low to the water table, and there can be found cranberry bogs with populations of carnivorous sundews, bog orchids, and other exotic and prehistoric-looking plants.

Another example of this shifting dune swale habitat is in the desert-like dunes among the undeveloped wilderness of Fire Island. Out in these dune-habitats on Fire Island there is a fresh-water aquifer pond and a nearby low, wet depression in the sand protected by a series of dunes from the Atlantic Ocean, which is less than 200 yards (183 meters) away. *Sphagnum* moss surrounds one side of this aquifer where sundews and cranberry grow, and there are other sundews growing in the wet sand of the nearby depression.

Much of the eastern landscape of Long Island is covered in what are known as pine barrens, with long stretches of mostly sand and nutrient-poor soils, pitch pines, and scrub oaks with little else to be noticed at first. The Peconic River runs through the heart of the central pine barrens, and the watershed along the river's sources and tributaries have created numerous bogs with live *Sphagnum* moss hummocks draped between Atlantic white cedar (*Chamaecyparis thyoides*) stands, with slow-moving water flowing through them. This is where the occasional populations of pitcher plants can be found. Commercial cranberry bogs once operated in these areas; long since abandoned, the foundations of their sluice gates still remain as worn pieces of concrete in linear stretches slowly being reclaimed by nature.

Intermittently scattered about the island and dotting its landscape are curiously isolated ponds that were formed from enormous chunks of ice left behind by the receding glaciers that originally created Long Island. The land buried these huge chunks of ice while they slowly melted, eventually forming sunken hollows that filled with water. Today they are known as coastal plains ponds, or more generally as "kettle holes." Coastal plains ponds are directly linked to the groundwater and fed by rainwater, their water levels fluctuating throughout the seasons and the years. Sometimes their gradually sloping shores are flooded under the water; other times, the shores are exposed to the open air. These habitats are sandy and nutrient poor and are full of communities of varied plant species that are specialized for these conditions, including the carnivorous sundews and bladderworts. The coastal plains ponds can be described as oases within the broad expanses of the dry, sandy landscape that is the pine barrens of this island.

Sand dune swale habitat.
June 15, 2013, iPhone 4 photograph

View to river from *Sphagnum* bog in Atlantic white cedar forest.
August 3, 2015, iPhone 5s photograph

Coastal plains pond habitat.
June 18, 2012, iPhone 4 photograph

Sundews

Sundews are known throughout much of the world, recognized by their ravenous traps covered in tentacles with what deceptively appear to be nectar dewdrops glistening in the sunlight. Three species of sundews grow native on Long Island; *Drosera intermedia*, *Drosera filiformis*, and *Drosera rotundifolia*. Each are discernible from one another, but *Drosera filiformis*, otherwise known as the threadleaf sundew, stands out in particular with its long and upright thread-like leaves that can approach nine inches in length and unfurl like those of a fern. *Drosera filiformis* is native to the eastern seaboard of the US and Canada in a few widely scattered and disjunctive populations from Nova Scotia to North Carolina, with more isolated populations on the panhandle of Florida. In New York, they are only found on the eastern part of Long Island in sandy soils that are moist and well drained. The habitats they occupy are mostly on the shorelines of coastal plains ponds or near other rain-fed pools of water that fluctuate throughout the seasons. Great populations of them are also seen in the dune swale habitats out towards the southeastern tip of the island on what is known as the South Fork. These habitats can sometimes be less than a thousand feet (305 meters) to the salt water of nearby bays, protected from the salt-spray air by the surrounding sand dunes.

The other two species, *Drosera rotundifolia*, commonly known as the roundleaf sundew, and *Drosera intermedia,* commonly known as the spoonleaf sundew, normally grow as rosettes and appear to be quite similar to one another, but can be told apart by a few particular characteristics. *Drosera rotundifolia* always grow as low rosettes having nearly circular-shaped traps and the leaf stems have varying degrees of bristles on them. The species can be common in the northern latitudes throughout the world from Europe through Siberia, to Japan and Korea, across northern America, and oddly even in the temperate mountains of New Guinea. It is also the most common sundew on Long Island and can be found all across the island in suitable habitats.

Drosera filiformis population in dune swale habitat.
June 15, 2013

Drosera filiformis
trap detail on coastal plains pond shoreline.
July 7, 2013

Drosera filiformis
flower in dune swale habitat.
July 7, 2013

Drosera intermedia are differentiated by their traps, which are much narrower than those of *Drosera rotundifolia* and so appear more spoon-like. The leaf stems are smooth and more rounded. Some *Drosera intermedia* plants even form long upright stalks in response to seasonal flooding and can grow relatively large in comparison. It is commonly found in other areas of the world as well, but it is not quite as widespread as *Drosera rotundifolia*. Seen in Europe and throughout eastern North America to around the Great Lakes in the US and Canada, it even grows as a tropical down in Cuba and northern South America. It is fairly common on Long Island as well, sometimes growing with *Drosera rotundifolia,* sometimes without.

The hybrid between *Drosera rotundifolia* and *Drosera intermedia,* known as *Drosera × belezeana,* has been discovered growing with both of the parent species in the live moss of a few *Sphagnum* bogs in the central pine barrens. This hybrid can be difficult to identify for it contains characteristics from both of the parents. The simplest way to tell the difference is that the traps are intermediate in shape, and the most visible features are a blending of the two species, not fully being one or the other. *Drosera × belezeana* is reported from other areas of the world where *Drosera rotundifolia* and *Drosera intermedia* grow together, such as in England, Germany, and France, in the provinces of Ontario and Nova Scotia in Canada, and also in the New Jersey Pine Barrens, New England, and Michigan in the US.

CLOCKWISE, FROM TOP LEFT

Drosera rotundifolia
colony on fallen Pitch–Pine tree
(Pinus rigida) lying across *Sphagnum* bog.
June 2, 2013

Drosera rotundifolia
plant in *Sphagnum* bog in Atlantic
white cedar forest.
June 22, 2013

Drosera rotundifolia
detail in *Sphagnum* bog in Atlantic
white cedar forest.
June 22, 2013

Drosera intermedia plant showing stem-forming
characteristic on sandy pond shore of coastal plains pond.
June 18, 2012

Drosera intermedia cluster of plants in habitat
of sandy pond shore of coastal plains pond.
August 1, 2015

Drosera intermedia detail in *Sphagnum* bog at edge of pond surrounded by cedar swamp.
August 24, 2014

Drosera × *belezeana* on floating *Sphagnum* mat.
July 28, 2015

Drosera × *belezeana* detail, on floating *Sphagnum* mat.
July 28, 2015

Drosera rotundifolia trap detail.
June 22, 2013

Drosera intermedia trap detail.
July 15, 2012

Drosera × *belezeana* trap detail.
August 24, 2014

Pitcher Plants

Sarracenia purpurea, more commonly known as the purple pitcher plant, is the most widespread of the North American pitcher plants and is instantly recognizable by its wide and squat, low-growing and tubby-bodied pitchers with high collar-like hoods protecting their mouths. Its entire territory spans across much of the eastern seaboard of the US up to the southeast of Canada, around the Great Lakes, and into central Canada. There are two recognized subspecies throughout this range: the northern subspecies, *Sarracenia purpurea* subsp. *purpurea*, and the southern subspecies, *Sarracenia purpurea* subsp. *venosa*, with Long Island near where their ranges diverge from one another. The purple pitcher plants are the only pitcher plants that are found on the island, and have great coloration when they grow in sunnier, more exposed places. In these cases, their colors are quite vivid, with deep venation of reds spreading across green backgrounds, sometimes being solid red on the entire body almost out to the fringes of the pitcher hood. The pitcher hoods are large, wavy, and fairly exaggerated with wide pitcher mouths that their hapless prey tumble down into. Interestingly, their pitcher bodies are often covered with short, soft hairs giving them a somewhat fuzzy, pubescent appearance more akin to the southern subspecies of these plants, while other traits they possess are more similar to the northern subspecies.

Long Island's pitcher plants are mostly seen growing in the live *Sphagnum* moss hummocks among Atlantic white cedar stands or in the peaty soils in which these trees grow. Other habitats where they grow are in meadow-like *Sphagnum* bogs not accompanied by the cedar trees or along the banks of rivers and tributaries, or even on large floating mats of *Sphagnum* moss in the center of ponds. Historically native across Long Island, *Sarracenia purpurea* unfortunately has been steeply declining in the past 100 years, being extirpated from all of their former western sites and disappearing from many of their eastern ones as well. Today they are only known to be in a few remaining locations in the vicinity of the Peconic River, and some of these are even tenuous at best.

Sarracenia purpurea plant on floating *Sphagnum* mat in pond.
July 28, 2015

Sarracenia purpurea trap detail in *Sphagnum* bog in Atlantic white cedar forest.
July 3, 2012

Bladderworts

The most diverse, widespread and complex of all the carnivorous plants are the species in the genus *Utricularia*, otherwise known as the bladderworts. Growing around the world as aquatics in still or slow-moving water, or as terrestrials in saturated soil where the water table is high, they can grow non-parasitically on other plants in rainforests as epiphytes, and sometimes even as lithophytes clinging to rocks in the faster moving water of streams and waterfalls. They have evolved miniature bladder-like traps that ingeniously create a vacuum inside of them to suck up their prey with incredible speeds when a trigger is tripped on their trap doors. The larger traps can range up to 0.47 inches (1.2 cm) and are visible floating in the water as aquatics where they usually capture prey such as water fleas (*Daphnia*), but sometimes will capture prey as large as mosquito larvae, small tadpoles, and even newborn fish, which are partially taken and then slowly consumed. The traps on the terrestrial bladderworts are normally much smaller, down to 0.008 inch (0.2 mm), and hidden underground catching tiny organisms, such as rotifers and other such multicellular creatures that swim through the waterlogged soils.

Usually the best way to identify the bladderworts is by their small, delicate flowers that rise up into the air and appear like miniature snapdragons or orchids, although their flowers can be so similar at times as to defy positive identification at first glance. Long Island has twelve species of native bladderworts and these different species grow and behave in some rather different ways. Some are found only floating in open water, others are affixed to the bottom of the shallows of ponds, and still others live rooted terrestrially.

The floating bladderworts are aquatic species that can become big, widely branching networks of stem-like structures known as stolons, which sprout out filamentous shoots; it is these types of plants that possess the largest of the carnivorous bladders. The purple-flowered eastern purple bladderwort (*Utricularia purpurea*) has a pale to reddish brown color to its branching networks and the purple flowers make it easily recognizable.

The other floating bladderworts of Long Island have yellow flowers, with the greater bladderwort (*Utricularia macrorhiza*) and the hidden fruit bladderwort (*Utricularia geminiscapa*) appearing to be very similar to one another. They can best be

Utricularia purpurea flower detail in coastal plains pond.
July 7, 2015

Utricularia striata
trap detail in coastal plains pond.
June 18, 2012

Utricularia striata
trap detail digesting prey in coastal plains pond.
June 18, 2012

differentiated when they go into flower. *Utricularia geminiscapa* creates an extra, downward-pointing flower scape underwater while *Utricularia macrorhiza* does not. The little floating bladderwort (*Utricularia radiata*) is another freely floating aquatic, which is easier to tell apart from the others. Clearly visible at the water's surface are horizontal radial floats that form spokes around the base of its flower stems, appearing like branching wheels.

Affixed aquatics grow in the shallower parts of ponds, rooted to the soil at the bottom where they send out strands of plumose growth to float upwards and hypnotically sway in the water when a gentle breeze blows by. Their "roots" are actually stolons that have many of the carnivorous bladder traps along them, capturing and digesting multitudes of minute subterranean denizens in the submerged substrate of sand and murk. Of these affixed aquatics, the flat-leaved bladderwort (*Utricularia intermedia*) and the lesser bladderwort (*Utricularia minor)* are similar to one another. These *Utricularia* both have little leaves along long stems that sprout out from the underwater soil, making them difficult to tell apart. These differences are so slim that it is better to identify them by their yellow flowers, of which *Utricularia minor* has a distinct, horizontally flat appearance in comparison to *Utricularia intermedia.*

Then there is the striped bladderwort (*Utricularia striata*), which is another affixed aquatic that grows anchored to the bottoms of ponds. This species has finely branching plumes that give the plants a foxtail appearance with fairly large aquatic traps visible on them; in contrast *Utricularia intermedia* and *Utricularia minor* have leafy plumes with all of their carnivorous bladders hidden underground.

Particularly confusing is the fact that the yellow flowers of the humped bladderwort (*Utricularia gibba*) look identical to those of *Utricularia striata*. Still, their growth forms and habits are very different. *Utricularia gibba* are noticeably smaller and have slender, branching stolons that often form dense mats. They are extremely adaptable and can float aquatically or sprawl through live *Sphagnum* moss or onto mucky soils but do not form the rooted foxtail-like plumes of *Utricularia striata* and are not nearly as robust.

Utricularia gibba
flower detail in *Sphagnum* bog at edge of pond
surrounded by cedar swamp.
August 10, 2013

Utricularia cornuta
flowers along coastal plains pond shoreline.
August 1, 2015

Utricularia resupinata
flower detail along coastal plains pond shoreline.
August 1, 2015

Utricularia cornuta
traps and stolons detail unearthed from sandy soil in shallow water along coastal plains pond shoreline.
July 22, 2012

In the shallowest of waters, or at the edge of the shores of ponds, or even in very wet sandy soils, grow the subaquatic, or semi-terrestrial, bladderworts. The horned bladderwort (*Utricularia cornuta*) and the similar rush bladderwort (*Utricularia juncea*) have yellow flowers that look very much the same. The main observable differences between these two species is that *Utricularia cornuta* has larger flowers that cluster near the top of the flower stalk, while *Utricularia juncea* has flowers that are smaller and are scattered along the length of the flower stalk. They both have stolons running horizontally underground that are dotted with their carnivorous traps. These stolons send out anchoring root-like shoots below, while long green shoots rise above the soil surface like miniature blades of grass.

Also growing in the shallow waters and creeping onto the wet mucky shores with underground carnivorous bladders is the lavender bladderwort (*Utricularia resupinata*), which on Long Island is only known to be found at two ponds that are adjacent to one another. The flowers of this little plant are a lavender color and have an unusual tell-tale shape like the letter C, which make them very unique.

Growing even more terrestrially in fully saturated sand is the zig-zag bladderwort (*Utricularia subulata*). These are perhaps the smallest of the local bladderworts, and they send out tiny yellow flowers on erect wiry scapes that sometimes have a zig-zag shape. The thin stolons grow underground sprouting carnivorous traps, while sending out narrow tapered leaves to photosynthesize above the soil. Bladderworts are such unusual plants and are completely fantastic. All of Long Island's native species of the bladderworts can also be found in other areas of the eastern seaboard of the US and some are even found across the world. Overall there are an estimated 230 species that exist today, with many more expected to be discovered as new areas of the world are explored and further studies are taken.

In these very same habitats where carnivorous plants grow, many other interesting plants are living alongside them as well. On the shores of the coastal plains ponds are natural habitats for unusual plants such as the meadow beauty (*Rhexia virginica*), rose coreopsis *(Coreopsis rosea)*, and the combleaf mermaidweed (*Proserpinaca pectinata*). Prehistoric-looking club moss (*Lycopodium appressum*) and bog orchids such as the grass pink (*Calopogon tuberosus*) can be seen in the dune swale habitats of the South Fork, and other bog orchids such as rose pogonia (*Pogonia ophioglossoides*) often inhabit many of the *Sphagnum* bogs of the central pine barrens where the purple pitcher plants grow.

Any excursion to view carnivorous plants in their natural habitats will certainly reveal amazing and beautiful places with rich ecosystems of unusual insects, reptiles, amphibians, and many other varieties of life. It can seem surprising to some that in the shadow of one of the world's largest megalopolis regions, and in an area more associated with suburban life, there can be such unaltered wilderness and interesting biodiversity. Yet here they are, continuing their fragile existence while the modern world steadily marches ever forward.

Epilogue

Carnivorous plants are widespread throughout the world and have been, in one form or another, for millions of years. Unfortunately today, many of these strange and remarkable plants are threatened with extinction from their natural habitats due to the pressures created by modern-day society.

Chief among these pressures is habitat destruction for housing and business development or for commercial plantations and agricultural use. The lands are drained, filled, and plowed over before the development begins, which completely obliterates the ecosystems and the life that once existed in them. In the southeast of the US, it is estimated that over 97.5 percent of the wetlands where carnivorous plants once existed have already been eradicated. This causes severe habitat fragmentation for the surviving populations that are cut off and isolated from one another when they are increasingly surrounded by developed areas. The surrounding land modifications interrupt the natural flow of water through the remaining ecosystems, causing the quality of these locations to stagnate steadily and degrade over time. Habitat fragmentation also often facilitates the spread of invasive species, which are difficult to eradicate once they begin to take hold. A slowly suffocating process, aggressive invasive species can eventually crowd the areas where carnivorous plants live, altering their habitats and eventually displacing them.

The suppression of natural forest fires is also quite detrimental. In many of the habitats where carnivorous plants exist, fires are a natural process that periodically clears the land of competing vegetation, and carnivorous plants are often adapted to these conditions.

In addition to these issues, the poaching of carnivorous plants is a particularly aggravating problem. People go into the few remaining healthy locations and illegally harvest the most vigorous specimens to sell them to commercial vendors, who, in turn, retail them to the public. This has the effect of removing not only the plants themselves, but also the hundreds or thousands of seeds each individual produces every season, further reducing the ability of the population to sustain itself. In one example of an effort to combat this problem, the State of North Carolina, where the Venus flytraps are native, recently enacted legislation to make it a felony to illegally collect these plants from the wild.

The dire risk of pollution to the ecosystems where carnivorous plants exist is another great concern. The days of factories dumping enormous amounts of untreated industrial waste into rivers and the wilderness are mostly in the past for the US and western Europe, but pollution is still a very serious issue, especially in the developing countries across the world. Pollution can also come from the runoff of rain, which collects and concentrates lawn fertilizers, pesticides, untreated sewage, and other waste from residential suburban neighborhoods and diverts them to the lower-laying wetlands, steadily creating toxic conditions within them. Individual homes may not create much of what is known as "non-point source pollution," but collectively, with millions of people, there can be some seriously detrimental effects on the local environments. These same freshwater habitats that carnivorous plants exist in are often necessary for maintaining the safe quality of the local drinking water in their respective regions, and so keeping these environments pristine and protected is in everyone's best interests.

Fortunately, there are a number of organizations working to stop the effects of these damaging pressures and are dedicated to the conservation of carnivorous plants and the habitats in which they exist.

The International Carnivorous Plant Society (carnivorousplants.org) is the place to begin for those who are interested in the conservation of carnivorous plants. Their websites have volumes of information and helpful internet links to learn more, and to answer many of the questions that might arise. The ICPS has contributed expertise and grants, and organized volunteer workers for a number of successful conservation projects. They also print and distribute the Carnivorous Plant Newsletter, which has reports of new discoveries, visits to

natural habitats, information on conservation projects, and other interesting news concerning carnivorous plants.

The International Union for Conservation of Nature (iucn.org) is the world's oldest and largest global environmental organization for conserving nature, managing field projects, supporting scientific research, and maintaining the definitive international standard for species extinction risk, the IUCN Red List of Threatened Species. They have a specialty carnivorous plant conservation group as well (iucn-cpsg.org).

The Nature Conservancy (nature.org) is the largest environmental conservation non-profit in the US and operates in 35 other countries protecting many land, fresh-water, and marine ecosystems from development. They also protect and manage some of the finest remaining carnivorous plant habitats in the US.

The North American Sarracenia Conservancy (nasc.org) is a non-profit volunteer conservation group for pitcher-plants and other carnivorous plants in the United States. They have partnered in the past with The Nature Conservancy and other organizations for conservation efforts in some of the most biodiverse and threatened habitats of carnivorous plants in the US.

Local volunteer nature conservation groups are also excellent opportunities for carnivorous plant enthusiasts to work within their local communities. Sometimes these efforts are more flexible for local projects and can also make significant contributions to projects of the larger organizations. This also affords the chance to meet and coordinate with other local individuals who share the interest in nature conservancy.

Over a relatively short period of time in history, modern-day society has altered the natural landscape of the earth drastically. We do have the ability to stem the tide of devastation, and assist in the restoration and proper management of the remaining suitable habitats for carnivorous plants, and in turn, for the other flora and fauna that depend on these same ecosystems. By doing our part to preserve the biodiversity of our world today, we help protect what will be left for the future generations of tomorrow and the ability of the Earth to sustain life as we know it.

Drosera intermedia
with prey capture of skimmer dragonfly on sandy pond shore of coastal plains pond.
June 18, 2012

Nepenthes 'The Succubus' cultivar
February 27, 2010

Plate Index

Dionaea muscipula, with the common name of the Venus flytrap, is found native in the sandy and peaty soils of bogs and wet savannahs only in North and South Carolina within a roughly sixty-mile radius of Wilmington, North Carolina. The conservation status of *Dionaea muscipula* is listed as Vulnerable on the International Union for Conservation of Nature (IUCN) Red List.

Dionaea muscipula; see Plate 01.
   This specimen is of the 'B52' cultivar, which was bred sometime before 2006 by Henning Von Schmeling and registered by Barry Rice in 2006.

Dionaea muscipula 'B52' cultivar; see Plate 01.

Drosera capensis is commonly known as the cape sundew, and occurs naturally in the southwestern Cape of South Africa, found in marshes, along streams, and in permanent seeps or damp areas of fynbos habitat. Although fairly uncommon, it is considered as not threatened in its natural habitat, which is quite remote and still undisturbed.

   Drosera prolifera, which is commonly known as the hen-and-chicks sundew, is endemic to Queensland, Australia, and typically grows in the densely shaded margins of the northeastern Australian rainforests in sandy soils along creek banks or on wet rocks near waterfalls. It is considered Vulnerable by the Parliament of Queensland in The Nature Conservation Act 1992.

Drosera binata, or the forked sundew, is a sundew species native to Australia and New Zealand. It occurs naturally in coastal areas from Fraser Island, south through New South Wales to Victoria and Tasmania. It can be fairly common in its natural habitat and so has not been evaluated for conservation status.
   This specimen is of the 'Marston Dragon' cultivar, which was described by Adrian Slack in 1986 and registered in 2001.

   Drosera regia is commonly known as the king sundew and is endemic to South Africa, having only ever been found in two sites along the Bainskloof Range near Wellington, Western Cape, in South Africa. At the higher-altitude site, they appear to have already been extirpated, and at the lower altitude site it is estimated that only about fifty mature plants survive, making *Drosera regia* extremely threatened with extinction from the wild. Unfortunately, this species has not been assessed by the IUCN Red List at this time.
   This specimen is of the 'Big Easy' cultivar, which was described and registered in 2004 by William Joseph Clemens.

Drosera regia; see Plate 08.

Drosera filiformis, known as the thread-leaf sundew, is native to a series of widely disjunctive populations along the eastern-Atlantic seaboard of North America, with a few populations on the Gulf-Coast of the Florida panhandle. This specimen is of an undescribed red variant that is distinct in that it colors pure red in the full sunlight it receives. The natural populations of this variant are found only in a small region of the Florida panhandle. This species has not been assessed by the IUCN Red List at this time.

Drosera adelae is commonly known as the lance-leaved sundew and is endemic to Queensland, Australia. This tropical plant typically grows in the densely shaded margins of the northeastern Australian rainforests in sandy soils along creek banks or on wet rocks near waterfalls. It is considered Rare by the Parliament of Queensland in The Nature Conservation Act 1992.

Pinguicula moranensis is a butterwort that has a range extending across areas of Mexico, Guatemala, and El Salvador. It grows in nutrient poor, alkaline soils on mossy banks, rocky cliff faces, and along roadsides in oak-pine, temperate mountain, or even tropical forests. This species has not been assessed by the IUCN Red List at this time.

PLATE 13 (page 27)
Supple flesh to ripple wet
October 21, 2012

Pinguicula moranensis; see Plate 12.

PLATE 14 (page 28)
Spite's singular purpose is revenge
October 21, 2012

Pinguicula reticulata is a butterwort from a range near the Sierra Madre Oriental mountains in Mexico. The species are found growing in the nutrient-poor soils on hillsides, along depressions, and in the rocky crevices of cliff faces. This species has not been assessed by the IUCN Red List at this time.

PLATE 15 (page 29)
What brings the viscous ooze
October 21, 2012

Pinguicula cyclosecta is a butterwort from a small range in the Sierra Madre Oriental mountains in Mexico. It is found on moss clinging to limestone rock walls, or in nutrient-poor soil collected in the crevices of these walls. This species has not been assessed by the IUCN Red List at this time.

PLATE 16 (pages 30–31)
Seething edge of chaos
February 15, 2014

Cephalotus follicularis has the common name of the Albany pitcher plant and is endemic to the coastal areas of extreme southwest Australia, where its habitat is on moist peaty sands found in swamps or along creeks and streams. The conservation status of the plants' populations in the wild is listed as Vulnerable on the IUCN Red List.

PLATE 17 (page 32)
Descent into the abyss
October 28, 2012

Cephalotus follicularis; see Plate 16.
This specimen is of the 'Hummer's Giant' cultivar, which was unofficially named sometime after 1986 and described and registered by John Hummer in 2000.

PLATE 18 (page 33)
The Moloch must be obeyed
February 15, 2014

Cephalotus follicularis; see Plate 16.

PLATE 19 (page 34)
Unseen grimace behind a faceless visage
October 28, 2012

Cephalotus follicularis, 'Hummer's Giant' cultivar; see Plate 16.

PLATE 20 (page 35)
Skulking intentions embodied in form
June 13, 2011

Darlingtonia californica is more commonly known as the cobra plant and is native to northern California and Oregon, growing in bogs, seeps, and stream banks that are fed by cold mountain water. While it is somewhat rare and its range limited, the plants are not under any immediate threat and so the conservation status of *Darlingtonia californica* is listed as a species of Least Concern on the IUCN Red List.

PLATES 21 AND 22 (pages 36 & 37)
Brutal obscene abominations
September 9, 2010

Sarracenia purpurea is commonly known as the purple pitcher plant, and its range includes much of the eastern seaboard of the United States, the Great Lakes, and southeastern to central Canada, making it the most common and broadly distributed species of the *Sarracenia*. They are found in habitats that tend to be poor in nutrients and acidic, such as in permanently wet bogs, fens, swamps, and grassy plains with exposure to strong sunlight. This specimen is of the southern subspecies *Sarracenia purpurea susp. venosa*. Although the species as a whole is widespread, the southern subspecies is under a lot of pressure from habitat development.

PLATES 23 AND 24 (pages 38 & 39)
False Promises
July 10, 2010

Sarracenia × *catesbaei* is the naturally occurring hybrid of *Sarracenia flava* and *Sarracenia purpurea* and can be found in the coastal plains region from Virginia to South Carolina, where its parent species coexist. The hybrids are found in the permanently moist and draining areas of swamps, lake edges, river banks, boggy pine forests, marl fens, water springs, and other low-lying areas. As it is a naturally occurring hybrid, it is not considered for evaluation for conservation status.

PLATES 25 AND 26 (pages 40 & 41)
Torches of insanity illuminate us all
September 17, 2011

Sarracenia leucophylla is also known as the white pitcher plant, and it inhabits moist and low-nutrient longleaf pine savannas along the United States Gulf Coast, in Mississippi, Alabama, along the Florida panhandle, and one remaining location in Georgia. Due to wide-scale destruction of its habitat, and over-collection for commercial sales, the conservation status of *Sarracenia leucophylla* is listed as Vulnerable on the IUCN Red List.

PLATE 27 (pages 42–43)
Thrusting turgid penetration
October 26, 2013

Sarracenia leucophylla; see Plates 25–26.

PLATE 28 (page 44)
Rapture
September 9, 2010

Nepenthes × dyeriana is the scientific name for a hybrid introduced under the coextensive cultivar name, *Nepenthes ×* 'Sir William T. Thiselton Dyer', which was named for the director of the Kew Botanical Gardens from 1885 to 1905. Bred by George Tivey of Veitch Nurseries, the plant was released in 1903. The parentage of *Nepenthes × dyeriana* is a complex cross between *N. × dicksonia (veitchii × rafflesiana) and N. × mixta (northiana × maxima).*

PLATE 29 (page 45)
Through the eyes of the voyeur
April 24, 2010

Nepenthes × dyeriana; see Plate 28.

PLATE 30 (page 46)
Quiet lurking for an exquisite ambush
September 18, 2010

Nepenthes eymae × (stenophylla × lowii) is a man-made horticultural hybrid of the female parent of *Nepenthes eymae*, which is endemic to the island of Sulawesi, crossed with the male parent of the naturally occurring hybrid *Nepenthes stenophylla × lowii*, which is endemic to the island of Borneo.

PLATE 31 (page 47)
Twisted grace
September 8, 2010

Nepenthes 'Ile de France' is a man-made hybrid that was bred by Yvon Vezier sometime before 1981 and named by Marcel Lecoufle before 1983. It was described by Adrian Slack in 1986, and the name was registered as a cultivar by Jan Schlauer in 2000. The parentage of *Nepenthes* 'Ile de France' is listed as a cross between the hybrid cultivar *N.* 'Effulgent Koto' *(mirabilis × thorelii)* and the hybrid of *N. × mixta (northiana × maxima).* Although it is very likely that the *N. thorelii* plant that was used for the *N.* 'Effulgent Koto' cultivar is actually *N. smilesii.*

PLATES 32 AND 33 (pages 48 & 49)
Obsessions of debauchery and the lecherous fantasies that accompany them
October 11, 2010

Nepenthes truncata × ephippiata is a man-made horticultural hybrid with the female parent of *Nepenthes truncata*, which is endemic to the Philippines, crossed with the male parent of *Nepenthes ephippiata*, which is endemic to the island of Borneo.

PLATES 34 AND 35 (pages 50 & 51)
The boundless appetite possessed by greed's gaping gullet
April 8, 2012

Nepenthes lowii is endemic to the island of Borneo on a number of isolated peaks in Sabah, northern Sarawak, and in Brunei. The plants are found in the nutrient-deficient soils of mossy forests and stunted ridge-top vegetation of the upper montane zone at altitudes from 5,413 feet (1,650m) to 8,530 feet (2,600m) above sea level, where they grow as both terrestrials and epiphytes. It is listed as Vulnerable on the IUCN Red List of Threatened Species.

PLATE 36 (page 52)
Immoral indulgences taste delicious
April 8, 2012

Nepenthes lowii; see Plates 34 and 35.

PLATE 37 (page 53)
Success through ruthless exploitation
September 18, 2010

Nepenthes ventricosa × (× trusmadiensis) is a man-made horticultural hybrid with the female parent of *Nepenthes ventricosa*, which is endemic to the Philippines, crossed with the male parent of *Nepenthes × trusmadiensis*, the natural hybrid of *Nepenthes lowii* and *Nepenthes macrophylla* from Mount Trus Madi on the island of Borneo.

PLATES 38 AND 39 (pages 54 &55)
The erotic nature of fear
June 5, 2011

Nepenthes hamata is endemic to the Indonesian island of Sulawesi, where it grows as a terrestrial, or epiphyte. This plant is found in the lower and upper montane mossy forests among scrub vegetation on mountain ridges and summits at elevations from 4,593 feet (1,400 m) to 8,200 feet (2,500 m) above sea level. It is listed as Vulnerable on the IUCN Red List.

PLATE 40 (page 56)
Untitled – *Nepenthes hamata* with photography studio armature
June 5, 2011; see Plates 38 and 39.

PLATE 41 (page 57)
Anarchy
June 5, 2011

Nepenthes hamata; see Plates 38 and 39.

PLATES 42 AND 43 (pages 58 & 59)
Haunting lamentations of beasts most foul
November 26, 2011

Nepenthes lowii × spectabilis is a man-made horticultural hybrid with the female parent of *Nepenthes lowii,* which is endemic to the island of Borneo, crossed with the male parent of *Nepenthes spectabilis,* which is endemic to the Indonesian provinces of North Sumatra and Aceh.

This specimen is the 'H. R. Giger' cultivar, which was described and registered by the author in March of 2015.

PLATES 44 AND 45 (pages 60 & 61)
Horns of wrath
November 9, 2013

Nepenthes lowii × spectabilis,
'H. R. Giger' cultivar;
see Plates 42 and 43.

PLATES 46 AND 47 (pages 62 & 63)
Beautifully grotesque
November 9, 2013

Nepenthes lowii × spectabilis,
'H. R. Giger' cultivar;
see Plates 42 and 43.

PLATE 48 (pages 64–65)
Scourge across the plains of Hades
November 9, 2013

Nepenthes lowii × spectabilis, 'H. R. Giger' cultivar; see Plates 42 and 43.

PLATE 49 (pages 66–67)
White hot fury
November 10, 2013

Nepenthes lowii × spectabilis, 'H. R. Giger' cultivar; see Plates 42 and 43.

PLATES 50 AND 51 (pages 68 & 69)
Voluptuous temptation in carnal bliss
May 13, 2012

Nepenthes lowii × ventricosa is a man-made horticultural hybrid with the female parent of *Nepenthes lowii,* which is endemic to the island of Borneo, crossed with the male parent of *Nepenthes ventricosa,* which is endemic to the Philippines.

This specimen is the 'The Succubus' cultivar, which was described and registered by the author in March of 2013.

PLATES 52 AND 53 (page 70 & 71)
Birth of something horrible
September 29, 2011

Nepenthes lowii × ventricosa,
'The Succubus' cultivar;
see Plates 50 and 51.

PLATES 54 AND 55 (pages 72 & 73)
Distorted perversions
May 3, 2014
Nepenthes lowii × ventricosa,
'The Succubus' cultivar;
see Plates 50 and 51.

PLATES 56 AND 57 (page 74 & 75)
Pulsing irresistible compulsions
June 3, 2015

Nepenthes lowii × veitchii is a man-made horticultural hybrid with the female parent of *Nepenthes lowii,* which is endemic to the island of Borneo, crossed with the male parent of *Nepenthes veitchii,* which is also endemic to the island of Borneo.

PLATE 58 (page 76)
Surge
June 1, 2015

Nepenthes lowii × veitchii; see Plates 56 and 57.

PLATE 59 (page 77)
Of unspeakable atrocities
June 2, 2015

Nepenthes lowii × veitchii; see Plates 56 and 57.

PLATE 60 (page 78)
Approach the wretched hollow
May 25, 2015

Nepenthes robcantleyi is endemic to the Philippines, from the island of Mindanao, growing in a terrestrial manner at an elevation of around 5,905 feet (1,800 m) above sea level. The one confirmed location has been cleared for logging, with no survivors left in the wild, while a second population has possibly been discovered in 2011 growing as epiphytes high in the trees. This species has not been assessed by the IUCN Red List at this time.

PLATE 61 (page 79)
Flowing luxurious pain
May 28, 2015

Nepenthes robcantleyi; see Plate 60.

PLATE 62 (pages 80–81)
Destiny matters little to the damned
May 28, 2015

Nepenthes robcantleyi; see Plate 60.

PLATE 63 (page 82)
Passage to forbidden pleasures
May 28, 2015

Nepenthes robcantleyi; see Plate 60.

PLATE 64 (page 83)
Ragged slit
May 26, 2015

Nepenthes robcantleyi; see Plate 60.

PLATES 65 AND 66 (pages 84 & 85)
Beware the hidden sacrifice in the promise of reward
May 25, 2015

Nepenthes robcantleyi; see Plate 60.

PLATES 67 AND 68 (pages 86 & 87)
Cast into the delightful pits of frenzied madness
June 3, 2013

Nepenthes × *trusmadiensis* is the natural hybrid of *Nepenthes lowii* and *Nepenthes macrophylla*. This hybrid is restricted to the narrow elevation band of between 8,200 feet (2,500 m) and 8,530 feet (2,600 m) above sea level on the summit ridge of Mount Trus Madi on the island of Borneo, where both of the parent species are sympatric. As it is a naturally occurring hybrid, it has not been considered for evaluation for conservation status.

PLATE 69 (page 88)
Rend
June 3, 2013

Nepenthes × *trusmadiensis*; see Plates 67 and 68.

PLATE 70 (page 89)
The Hole
July 6, 2015

Nepenthes × *trusmadiensis*; see Plates 67 and 68.

PLATES 71 AND 72 (pages 90 & 91)
Butcher's adoration
July 6, 2015

Nepenthes × *trusmadiensis*;
see Plates 67 and 68.

PLATE 73 (page 92)
Ethereal machinations from beyond the grave
May 4, 2014

Utricularia sandersonii is a bladderwort endemic to South Africa, where it usually grows as a lithophyte clinging to wet, vertical rock faces at elevations between 689 feet (210 m) and 3,937 feet (1,200 m). This specimen is of a form that consistently produces flowers with a blue-purple color as opposed to the white color normally seen in this species. Its conservation status is listed as a species of Least Concern on the IUCN Red List.

PLATE 74 (page 93)
The hazy mist of lethargy creeps
November 8, 2015

Utricularia calycifida is a bladderwort endemic to northern South America in Brazil, Guyana, Suriname, and Venezuela, where it is normally found in shaded wet areas in forest or open savanna and sometimes on rocks exposed to waterfall spray. Unfortunately, this species has not been assessed by the IUCN Red List at this time. This specimen is of the 'Asenath Waite' cultivar, which was created in 2000 and described and registered by Barry Rice in 2001.

PLATE 75 (pages 94–95)
Fluttering movements in the elegant dance with death
September 30, 2012

Dionaea muscipula; see Plate 01.

Acknowledgments

For those of whose input and efforts helped make this book possible:

Marcel Van der Broek, president, International Carnivorous Plant Society, for all his inexhaustible help in reviewing, commenting, and constructive criticism of the initial material.

Peter D'Amato, owner of California Carnivores and author of *The Savage Garden,* for his foreword and the inspiration and encouragement in my early days of cultivation through to today.

Steve Young, chief botanist, New York Natural Heritage Program, for all of the information, input, and feedback on the natural habitats of Long Island's carnivorous plants.

Barry Rice, CPN Science Editor, for his advice, reviewing, and feedback on native carnivorous plants and conservation.

Jan Schlauer, cultivar registrar ICPS, CPN science editor, for review and feedback on the carnivorous plant taxonomy and cultivars.

Joel Koos, for creating the graphic for the map of The Outer Lands.

Jessica Koos, for writing the author's biography.

Natalie Jovic for photograph of the author on book jacket.

Eric Lamont, president, Long Island Botanical Society, for the volumes of information on the locations and habitats of Long Island's carnivorous plants.

Jim Ash, vice president of the board of directors, South Fork Natural History Museum, for personally showing me some of Long Island's greatest carnivorous plant habitats and fostering a greater appreciation for the other plants and animals within those habitats.

Les Barany, agent to H. R. Giger., for all his help and encouragement in getting this ambitious project off the ground and into process

Robert Zeimer, editor, International Carnivorous Plant Society, for all of his help and patience in editing the CPN articles I authored, which led to my ability to attempt this endeavor.

Yasmin Tayag, co-founder, Sci-Art Center, for her help in reviewing and feedback of initial material.

Further Reading

BOOKS

Bogs of the Northeast by Charles W. Johnson. In-depth and invaluable information on the greater region that Long Island belongs to and on the ecosystems that carnivorous plants can be found in. University Press of New England, 1985.

Carnivorous Plants of the United States and Canada by Donald Schnell. Great detailed source of information on the carnivorous plants that are native to the US and Canada, including those found on Long Island, NY. Timber Press, 2002.

Field Guide to the Carnivorous Plants of the United States and Canada by Stewart McPherson and Donald Schnell. Great source of information on the carnivorous plants in the US and Canada, including those found on Long Island, NY. Redfern Natural History Productions, Ltd., 2013.

Growing Carnivorous Plants by Barry A. Rice. Excellent resource of the cultivation of carnivorous plants and their habitat conservation, with excellent photography. Timber Press, 2006.

The Savage Garden: Cultivating Carnivorous Plants by Peter D'Amato. The most complete overview and in-depth information on the home cultivation of carnivorous plants with conservation information including numerous beautiful photographs. Ten Speed Press, 2013. More information at californiacarnivores.com.

The Outer Lands: A Natural History Guide to Cape Cod, Martha's Vineyard, Nantucket, Block Island, and Long Island by Dorothy Sterling. Artistic, flowing narrative overview of Long Island and its surrounding islands, the habitats and ecosystems that exist within them, and the plants and animals that are a part of them. W. W. Norton & Co., 1978, revised.

In addition, **Redfern Publishing** specializes in books about carnivorous plants in their natural habitats from across the entire globe, with volumes of titles on many different subjects. See redfernnaturalhistory.com.

WEBSITE LINKS

www.dec.ny.gov The homepage of the New York State Department of Environmental Conservation. Contains information about the New York Natural Heritage Program, which is an excellent starting point for information on nature in New York State and on Long Island.

Mkaelin.com Author's website. Contains more of the author's work including exhibition photographs, photograph print proofs, curriculum vitae, and more details on the native carnivorous plant populations on Long Island, New York.

Sarracenia.com Website by Barry A. Rice. Volumes of information and tips for the cultivation of carnivorous plants and about their natural habitats, with great photography and particulars of their taxonomy.

PUBLISHED ARTICLES BY THE AUTHOR

"International Carnivorous Plant Society 2012 Conference Field Trip," *International Carnivorous Plant Society Newsletter* 43, no. 2 (June 2014). Field report in narrative format on observations of ecologies and specimens in natural habitats at various locations around Wilmington, North Carolina.

"The Life and Death of Arthur Dobbs," *International Carnivorous Plant Society Newsletter,* 43, no. 3, (September 2014). History, accomplishments, and legacy of Arthur Dobbs, the person who discovered *Dionaea muscipula*, otherwise known as the Venus Flytrap.

"New Cultivars, 'H.R. Giger,'" *International Carnivorous Plant Society Newsletter* 45, no. 1 (March 2014). Description and naming of an exceptional specimen of the hybrid *Nepenthes lowii x spectabilis* as the cultivar 'H.R. Giger.'

"New Cultivars, 'The Succubus'" *International Carnivorous Plant Society Newsletter* 42, no. 1 (March 2013). Description and naming of an exceptional specimen of the hybrid *Nepenthes lowii x ventricosa red* as the Cultivar 'The Succubus.'

"The Sundew Hybrid *Drosera x belezeana* Found on Long Island, New York,*" International Carnivorous Plant Society Newsletter* 43, no. 3 (September 2014). Discovery of the hybrid *Drosera x belezeana* on Long Island, New York. Description of the hybrid and characteristics of the habitat.

Index

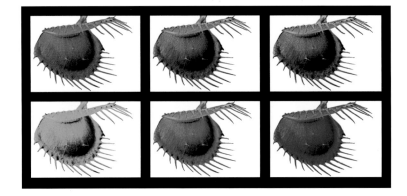

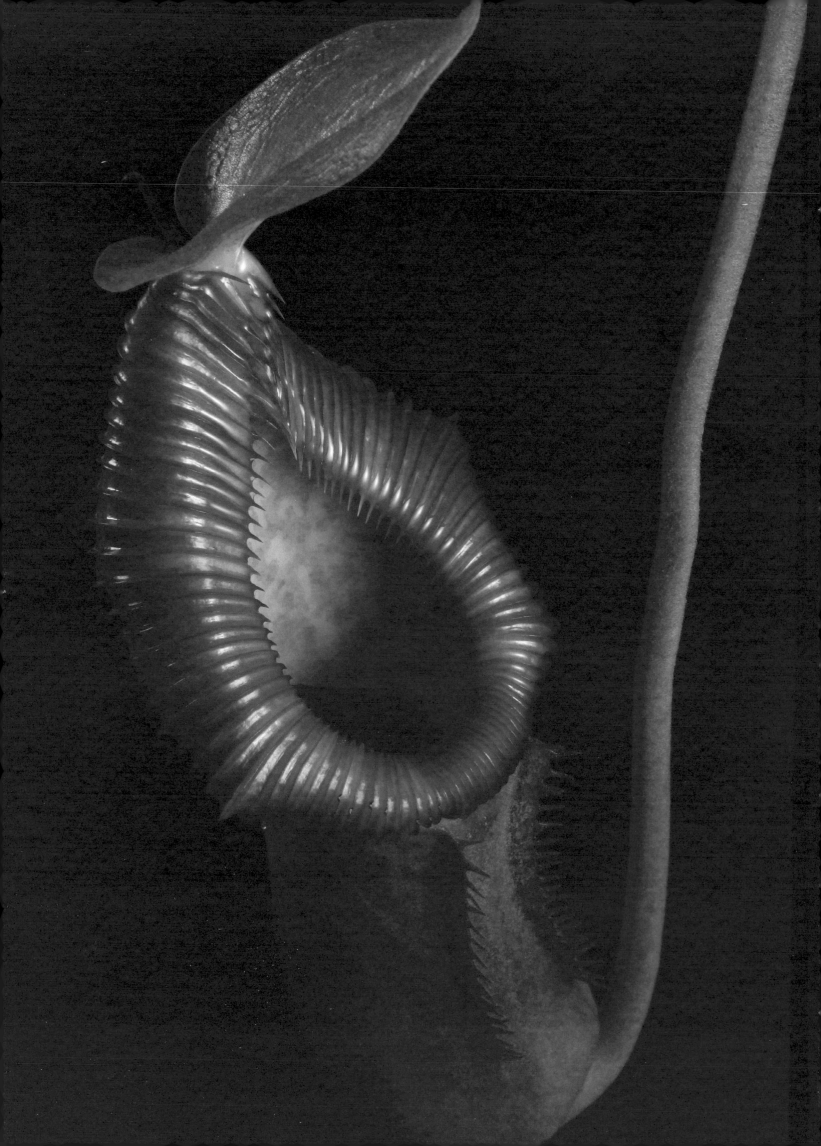